I Hear The Rocks Falling
Rev Kathryn L. Smith

Author of
There Is Fire In The Blood and Meet Me On The Mountain

I Hear The Rocks Falling.
Rev. Kathryn L. Smith
Author of There Is Fire In The Blood, Meet Me On The Mountain and I Hear The Rocks Falling.

Copyright © Kathryn L. Smith
May, 2017

Published By Parables
May, 2017

All Rights Reserved. No part of this book may be reproduced or utilized in any form or by any means, electronic or mechanical, including photocopying, recording, or by any information storage and retrieval system, without permission in writing from the author.

Unless otherwise specified Scripture quotations are taken from the authorized version of the King James Bible.

    ISBN 978-1-945698-26-2
    Printed in the United States of America

Readers should be aware that Internet Web sites offered as citations and/or sources for further information may have been changed or disappeared between the time this was written and when it is read.

I Hear
The Rocks Falling
Rev Kathryn L. Smith

Author of
There Is Fire In The Blood and Meet Me On The Mountain

Kathryn L. Smith

Table of Contents

5	Foundation Stones
9	She Heard the Stones Falling
15	Bathsheba and I
21	And The Walls Fell Down
27	Stones from the Past
39	Living in the Rubble
47	Altar Stones
53	Mizpah
59	Tower of Babble
67	Stones in the Jordan
73	They Could Have Stoned Her
79	Roll Away the Stone
87	The Hard Road
95	Beaten, Stoned, Free
103	Striking the Rock
111	Are the Rocks Crying Out
115	Works Cited
116	Author Page

KATHRYN L. SMITH

Acknowledgements

It is with deep love that I dedicate this book to my wonderful husband, William R. Smith II, [Buzz]. I feel a very deep gratitude for his unwavering support. He has loved me all these years and allowed me to follow God's call, even when it meant I was gone preaching or consumed with writing.

I deeply appreciate all those who made me the woman of faith, the minister, and the author that I am. I want to especially thank my Pastor Timothy A. Naylor, and those previous Pastors who have guided and instructed me over the years. I want to honor Pastor Rick Naylor, who taught me what it meant to be called and how to minister. He taught me faith, and to trust in the indisputable Word of God. These men of faith invested in my spiritual growth and served as shepherds to my soul. I also want to express my gratitude to the men and women whose ministries and books have shaped my faith; some of those names have faded over time, but their truths have become ingrained within my spirit; to all those who taught me and nurtured me, but were not specifically cited in this book—thank you.

I also want to thank the people who so kindly and consistently encouraged me, and those who have purchased and read my books. I wish to thank Donna Naylor who was the first to read each of my books and who graciously did some editing. She helped me with grammar and punctuation, while always honoring the message within the text.

Mostly, I want to thank the Lord Jesus Christ who loved me when I was unlovely, saved me when I was lost, called me when I was nothing and anointed me to do His work. I pray that He will be glorified and lifted high in all I have attempted for Him.

Romans 8:1-2 (KJV) *1 There is therefore now no condemnation to them which are in Christ Jesus, who walk not after the flesh, but after the Spirit. 2 For the law of the Spirit of life in Christ Jesus hath made me free from the law of sin and death.*

Foundation Stones

I have been told that it was an odd, but interesting title, *I Hear The Rocks Falling*. After all, rocks are just solid hardened bits of earth. They are minerals and clay and sand that get compressed over time. Some are deemed valuable by mankind; we call those gemstones. Most are just common rock found lying about and aren't worth much. There is not much value in dirt and gravel unless you have to put in a driveway. We use various forms of rock and stone for paving, headstones and foundation stones and even jewelry, but they are still just dirt. Actually they have the same chemical make up as you and me.

God made Adam from the clay. He was just another thing made of dirt like the bits of stones lying on the ground around him. He too, was just a hard, dry, dead shell of a thing until the breath of God filled him. **Genesis 2: 7 (KJV)** *7 And the LORD God formed man of the dust of the ground, and breathed into his nostrils the breath of life; and man became a living soul.* That breath of "God life" differentiated man from all of creation. God put His own life within us, and we are all living on that borrowed breath the whole time we are here on earth. How many times have we heard, 'Ashes to ashes and dust to dust?' Every man returns to the ground from which he came. **Genesis 3:19 (KJV)** *... till thou return unto the* *ground; for out of it wast thou taken: for dust thou art, and unto dust shalt thou return.* When the World Trade Centers fell, the dust from cement was not easily distinguishable from the ashes of the people incinerated in the rubble. We are all a part of this earth, and yet we look at it and think ourselves different.

When I looked in the Book of Genesis, and read about creation. I could not find a specific reference to God creating stone or rock. The garden seems to have been all soft and pliable soil, and it was created to bring forth life, to produce. Once soil has hardened into stone, it is pretty much useless for planting and farming. I can see the value of stones for shelter and later for both tools and weapons, but it was unnecessary in the Garden.

This book is not so much about the kind of rocks we see as it is the things they represent or the walls we have built from them. There are accounts where I am literally talking about stones, rocks poised to be hurled at some lost soul like the woman caught in adultery. How sad that something taken from the earth would be used to try to destroy God's greatest treasure in the earth. Sometimes there were others, who like her, could have been stoned. What a relief it must have been when the accused and condemned heard the sound of those rocks gathered for destruction drop to the ground one by one.

There are also the more figurative stone walls of pride and sin and fear that mankind builds to hide behind only to realize they have created a prison. Remembering the past can shape our future for the good, or it can lock us into a place as real as any dungeon. We must never let the past rob us of our future. We cannot let our failures and mistakes ensnare and confine us. We can never allow condemnation to hold us prisoner; it was defeated at the cross. **Romans 8:1-2 (KJV)** *1 There is therefore now no condemnation to them which are in Christ Jesus, who walk not after the flesh, but after the Spirit. 2 For the law of the Spirit of life in Christ Jesus hath made me free from the law of sin and death.* In many ways this book is about coming out of our individual prison walls and hearing the sound of freedom as those walls start tumbling down.

There are also stones set up as memorials—engraved with names and dates we want to remember. Those places are intentionally set up as something that seems permanent, enduring and strong enough to keep a memory alive. Hopefully those towers and headstones and monuments do not confine us to that time and place, but rather mark our progress through life.

There are some stones that we need to hear crumble and fall to the ground to set us free from the prisons that bind us to the place where we got stuck and walled off from people and sometimes even from God. It is my desire that by the time you have finished reading, you will hear the rocks falling.

John 8:10-11 *¹⁰ When Jesus had lifted up himself, and saw none but the woman, he said unto her, Woman, where are those thine accusers? hath no man condemned thee? ¹¹ She said, No man, Lord. And Jesus said unto her, Neither do I condemn thee: go, and sin no more.*

She heard The Stones Falling

In the Bible to stone someone was to pelt them with stones or rocks until dead. I always thought of that being smaller rocks, but in fact it was mostly large heavy stones used to crush the head or tear the flesh of the guilty until they died. Larger stones would not be thrown from far away, but were brought near and hurled or dropped upon the condemned. What a terrible scene. When they stoned people in ancient times, they took the same substance from which God made mankind, and used it to kill and destroy them. How sad, that the earth itself could be used to snuff out the life of God once breathed into a clay shell of man. It was a painful way to die, and was generally seen as a judgment from the whole community. Sometimes even children hurled smaller rocks at the condemned. It is the way Steven died. [Acts 6:11-7:60] One version of the Bible says the murderous stones rained down upon him. His crime was not that of a thief or anything that harmed others, he died because he was a true believer in Christ. This was not the case of everyone who was stoned, and certainly not the case of our adulterous woman.

John 8:1-3 (KJV) *1 Jesus went unto the mount of Olives.* He went to a place of solitude and frequently his place of prayer, and having just left the Father, He goes to the temple to teach. *2 And early in the morning he came again into the temple, and all the people came unto him; and he sat down, and taught them.* The Temple courtyard was a very public place with a large crowd. It was a holy place, basically their church. Here the righteous were gathered, and singing and reading the Old Testament scriptures. Here they shared their faith, entered into the community of Jewish believers; coming here was part of their normal way of life. It was a safe place, a good place. The teacher is opening truth to them. It is safe to say that there were hundreds gathered there. *3 And the scribes and Pharisees brought unto him a woman taken in adultery; and when they had set her in the midst,* They broke into her bedroom and dragged her into a place crowded with people, religious people—good people, and there is a drastic difference between this woman and everyone around her. She is truly guilty, full of shame and distress. In the midst of these men, her sin screams into the silence of the temple courtyard. Everyone stares at her and her tear-filled eyes look only at the ground. She has no defense; she can say nothing to placate their hatred and anger. Her sin can no longer be hidden or denied, but is now on public display.

To be taken in the act of adultery, she had to be trapped or targeted. She had to be ripped from her bed; she was probably not fully clothed. She has to feel betrayed and naked on so many levels. Here she is with no excuse; she cannot make a case for mercy. She is guilty and they all know it. **John 8:3-5 (KJV)** *3 And the scribes and Pharisees brought unto him a woman taken in adultery; and when they had set her in the midst, 4 They say unto him, Master, this woman was taken in adultery, in the very act. 5 Now Moses in the law commanded us, that such should be stoned: but what sayest thou?* It is true that she sinned. It is also true that if found guilty of breaking the Mosaic Law by the Jewish leaders, she could be sentenced to death. But, that law included the death of her lover, who seems to be missing. The law was taken out of context, and it was a law that no one literally enforced at that time. They used it to trap not only the woman but Jesus as well. If He says let her go, He insults and rejects the Law of Moses, and the religious will see

Him as unrighteous. If He says kill her, He is going against His own teachings on love and grace, and also He is issuing a death sentence which was a power reserved for the Governor according to Roman law in this occupied territory. Only Jesus stands between her and sure death. He willingly stood there, between her and her accusers, the same way He does for us. His shadow covered her and His form shielded her from their stares.

John 8:6-7 *6 This they said, tempting him, that they might have to accuse him. But Jesus stooped down, and with his finger wrote on the ground, as though he heard them not.* Roman judgment came with a written indictment from which the sentence would be pronounced. Maybe He wrote, "Caught in adultery" or, maybe He was symbolically making a statement that their accusations had no more substance than what was written in the sand—easily blown away. Maybe Jesus was just shifting the horrible stares from the woman to His own frame as He bent to write in the dust. Maybe He was writing the real law from the books of Moses. Many believe He was listing their individual sins. I can imagine Jesus scrawling the words hypocrite, thief, liar, pedophile, idolater, prideful and even murderer in the dirt. In any case, Jesus was ignoring their shouts of accusation and that infuriated them. *7 So when they continued asking him, he lifted up himself, and said unto them, He that is without sin among you, let him first cast a stone at her.* That may be exactly what He wrote; His verdict. 'The truly innocent may judge and kill this woman.' The Romans wrote out their findings and read the death sentence from a scroll as their laws demanded. Even in America, our court system has the foreman read the findings of the jury in open court. Perhaps Jesus was writing His righteous judgement out there in the dirt. None of us knows for sure what He wrote, but we do know that He did nothing without a purpose.

John 8:8-9 *8 And again he stooped down, and wrote on the ground. 9 And they which heard it, being convicted by their own conscience,* When we heard the Gospel and really understood it, when the truth pricked our hearts and we felt the need for Him, then we understood our sins were evil. It was only then, that we were ready for grace. Once aware of ones guilt, the response is either to flee or to repent. Those who so quickly judged this woman felt the shame of their own frailties, failures and sins. As they did, it troubled and convicted them until they slipped away. *9 And they which heard it, being convicted by their own conscience, went out one by one beginning at the eldest, even unto the last: and Jesus was left alone, and the woman standing in the midst.* The voices in the mob grew more and more quiet, and she heard the first stone drop to the ground. She wondered if someone threw it and missed. She was still trembling with fear. How long until she felt the blows? One by one, 'thud' another accuser drops his stone. She hears the rocks falling over and over, the same stones meant to destroy her. Thud—thud. Those stones were meant to be thrown at her crushing her bones and bruising and cutting her flesh. But instead, they are dropped. There is another dull thump. She does not understand but she is thankful no one has hit her. There are footsteps as the men who came in their self-righteousness walk away, themselves convicted and ashamed. The youngest leaves last, his stone falling to the ground near Jesus. I can almost see the Lord glance up from the ground and picking up one of the stones, hold it out to each of the ones in the distance that had come to hear him teach. They too shake their heads no, recognizing that they had sin in their lives and none had the right to stone her.

Every time she heard one of those stones fall to the ground, condemnation and death were falling away from her. Guilt and fear were less heavy in her heart, but she was not free just yet.

John 8:10-11 *10 When Jesus had lifted up himself, and saw none but the woman, he said unto her, Woman, where are those thine accusers? hath no man condemned thee?* 'Where are all those who ripped you from your bed and dragged you through the streets and brought you to the house of God to accuse you? Where are those who determined to kill you?' *11 She said, No man, Lord.* In my mind Jesus reaches down and takes her hand to help her rise. *And Jesus said unto her, Neither do I condemn thee: go, and sin no more.*

If there was a stone in His hand, Jesus could have thrown it. He alone was sinless. But He let judgment fall to the ground. *Neither do I condemn thee: go, and sin no more*—I will not judge you. Jesus never said she was innocent or that sin did not matter. His actions said that His love was greater than her sin. His mercy was enough, and His blood was enough. Sin requires punishment, the guilty must face the consequence of their rebellion and it demands justice. Scripture tells us sin comes at a high price. **Romans 6:23 (KJV)** *23 For the wages of sin is death; but the gift of God is eternal life through Jesus Christ our Lord.* **Hebrews 9:22 (NIV)** *22 In fact, the law requires that nearly everything be cleansed with blood, and without the shedding of blood there is no forgiveness.* There is no higher price—a life must be given. She thought she would die that day, die in her sin, but Jesus was willing to be her redeemer, to assume her debt, and yours and mine. He carried that very sin to the cross.

His love was more than she or I had earned. It was more than I deserved, and it was not based upon my behavior. His grace and love were a foregone conclusion. He chose to love me when I did not deserve it. **1 John 4:17-19 (KJV)** *17 Herein is our love made perfect, that we may have boldness in the day of judgment: because as he is, so are we in this world. 18 There is no fear in love; but perfect love casteth out fear: because fear hath torment. He that feareth is not made perfect in love. 19 We love him, because he first loved us.*

John was among the Lord's inner circle of disciples, His dear friend. He was with Jesus on the Mount of Transfiguration. He was among the three who went in when Jairus' daughter was raised from the dead and among those praying with Jesus at Gethsemane. John never said I am the one who loves Jesus. He constantly called himself the disciple whom Jesus loved. Knowledge of that deep unconditional love made John the man he was. It was John who recorded the event we have been focused on and also the best known of all scriptures. **John 3:16 (KJV)** *16 For God so loved the world, that he gave his only begotten Son, that whosoever believeth in him* *should not perish, but have everlasting life.* John understood what the woman caught in adultery experienced and what every last sinner needed to know. Love and compassion are greater than sin. A cross and a tomb were determined for all of us. Hell was our final destination, the result of original sin and by our own actions, but Jesus stood between us and sure death. He got between us and the nails and the stones and every other instrument of death. Jesus loved so deeply, that He poured out the life blood within Him to free us from the hold of death and the fear of death and the dread of standing before a Holy God. Perfect love cast out fear, so mercy could be shown.

That nameless woman in the Bible walked away from the penalty of her sin, and more importantly, walked free from the guilt and shame of it. When Jesus deals with our sins it is never for the purpose of embarrassment or condemnation, but it is an opportunity to walk away free. **John 8:36 (KJV)** *36 If the Son therefore shall make you free, ye shall be free indeed.* It is our Lord and Savior who said, "Neither do I condemn thee: go, and sin no more."

Bathsheba and I

My public disgrace came in the spring of 1971. I know how that woman caught in adultery felt. At seventeen I faced my parents and told them that I was pregnant. There was the same sense of worthlessness. They never once even considered that I had been date raped by the man who they just considered my boyfriend. The same man, who asked me to marry him, told me to have an abortion. There was no mercy, no offer of grace, just that I got caught in my promiscuity and the undeniable truth that I was going to have a baby, alone, without support. I felt used, damaged, dirty, broken and rejected. I felt judged by almost everyone. If I knew the Bible back then I would have related my pain, my guilt, my predicament to that of Bathsheba.

2 Samuel 11:2-5 (KJV) *2 And it came to pass in an eveningtide, that David arose from off his bed, and walked upon the roof of the king's house: and from the roof he saw a woman washing herself; and the woman was very beautiful to look upon. 3 And David sent and enquired after the woman. And one said, Is not this Bathsheba, the daughter of Eliam, the wife of Uriah the Hittite?* She is the daughter of your friend and the wife of your trusted soldier. Neither of those facts restrained him from calling her to his bedchamber. *4 And David sent messengers, and took her; and she came in unto* *him, and he lay with her; for she was purified from her uncleanness: and she returned unto her house. 5 And the woman conceived, and sent and told David, and said, I am with child.*

David took Bathsheba into his bed. He was the king and he could have anyone he wanted. He already had seven wives and many concubines, but he wanted Bathsheba. This married woman, either with or without her own desire, surrendered to his lust. Then she found herself carrying the child of adultery. She found herself in a place where her guilt was public, while his was covered by the shadows. His guilt was no less than hers, but David was the king. Who would ever accuse him? So, she waits in fear, while he plots from his superior place of authority, not to repent, but to hide the sin that resulted in her pregnancy.

2 Samuel 11:6-15 (KJV) *6 And David sent to Joab, saying, Send me Uriah the Hittite. And Joab sent Uriah to David. 7 And when Uriah was come unto him, David demanded of him how Joab did, and how the people did, and how the war prospered. 8 And David said to Uriah, Go down to thy house, and wash thy feet. And Uriah departed out of the king's house, and there followed him a mess of meat from the king.* If Uriah just sleeps with his wife one time, the sin could be hidden, suspicions silenced. *9 But Uriah slept at the door of the king's house with all the servants of his lord, and went not down to his house. 10 And when they had told David, saying, Uriah went not down unto his house, David said unto Uriah, Camest thou not from thy journey? why then didst thou not go down unto thine house? 11 And Uriah said unto David, The ark, and Israel, and Judah, abide in tents; and my lord Joab, and the servants of my lord, are encamped in the open fields; shall I then go into mine house, to eat and to drink, and to lie with my wife? as thou livest, and as thy soul liveth, I will not do this thing. 12 And David said to Uriah, Tarry here today also, and tomorrow I will let thee depart. So Uriah abode in Jerusalem that day, and the morrow. 13 And when David had called him, he did eat and drink before him; and he made him drunk: and at even he went out to lie on his bed with the servants of his lord, but went not down to his house. 14 And* *it came to pass in the morning, that David wrote a letter to Joab, and sent it by the hand of Uriah.* David's plan had failed, Uriah had too much integrity to sleep with his wife, so David's back up plan is to have him killed and he has Uriah carry his own death sentence back to the battlefield. *15 And he wrote in the letter, saying, Set ye Uriah in the forefront of the hottest battle, and retire ye from him, that he may be smitten, and die.*

Meanwhile, Bathsheba lives in constant fear and dread. You can't hide pregnancy for long. The Law of Moses demanded that an adulteress be put to death. She imagined the torture of seeing such hatred and disappointment in the eyes of her family and friends as they judged her a harlot, and stoned her to death. She must have imagined a mob closing in around her, taking up stones to destroy her and the tiny life within her. She took no real joy from the child within her; she could not rejoice over him. Since her husband, Uriah, had been gone to battle for months, she could not have conceived by him. Her sin was about to be exposed and rather than admitting his own guilt, David tried to hide his sin by making it possible that Uriah had fathered a child that was born a bit early. That must have been another wound to her soul, that David would even consider putting her in that place where she would be lying to her husband while carrying this child of adultery. I am sure that she feared for her life, and while David assured her that the stones would never touch her. He did not know that he had caused her to feel more damaged, shattered, and broken than any rocks could have. He had taken her, either by force or even willingly, into his bed and then he had treated her like a harlot, sending her away as if the night they spent together meant nothing. He had nothing to say to her until she came up pregnant and then he had to act.

When Uriah had too much integrity to enjoy his marriage bed while his men were in the fields fighting a war, David ordered him killed. So now, in a sense, both of them have murdered him. If she wasn't already wallowing in shame and regret and dread, if she did not feel great judgment before surely the widow with the baby bump does now. **2 Samuel 11:26-27 (KJV)** *26 And when the wife* *of Uriah heard that Uriah her husband was dead, she mourned for her husband. 27 And when the mourning was past, David sent and fetched her to his house, and she became his wife, and bare him a son. But the thing that David had done displeased the LORD.*

Even when she is brought to the king, and married, everyone knows she came there already carrying the child. None of his other wives welcomed her—the fact that she is there at all says they weren't enough for him. There is jealously and hatred and she has to feel shunned. David does not call her to his chamber, because a king must build a strong family so the other wives service him while she is pregnant, alone, and despised. She is living imprisoned by her sin and shame right there in the palace. Even when her son is born, and she cherishes him, the judgment of God seems to rain down on her. The Bible did not even name the poor babe.

2 Samuel 12:7-14 (KJV) *7 ... Thus saith the LORD God of Israel, I anointed thee king over Israel, and I delivered thee out of the hand of Saul; 8 And I gave thee thy master's house, and thy master's wives into thy bosom, and gave thee the house of Israel and of Judah; and if that had been too little, I would moreover have given unto thee such and such things. 9 Wherefore hast thou despised the commandment of the LORD, to do evil in his sight? thou hast killed Uriah the Hittite with the sword, and hast taken his wife to be thy wife, and hast slain him with the sword of the children of Ammon.* David murdered Uriah. In the eyes of God it was as if he held the sword in his own hand. *10 Now therefore the sword shall never depart from thine house; because thou hast despised me, and hast taken the wife of Uriah the Hittite to be thy wife... 13 And David said unto Nathan, I have sinned against the LORD. And Nathan said unto David, The LORD also hath put away thy sin; thou shalt not die. 14 Howbeit, because by this deed thou hast given great occasion to the enemies of the LORD to blaspheme, the child also that is born unto thee shall surely die.* Judgment fell on the child of adultery, the parents were guilty, but the prophet says the child gave a place for Israel's enemies to dishonor to the Lord. David's adultery brought criticism to the throne and to the one true God he pledged to honor.

After all that Bathsheba has suffered, she gives birth to a baby who then dies. It seems there is no end to her misery. It is at this point that David repented. We can see his deep sorrow as he pours out his heart in the Psalms. **Psalm 51:1-17 (KJV)** *1 Have mercy upon me, O God, according to thy lovingkindness: according unto the multitude of thy tender mercies blot out my transgressions. 2 Wash me throughly from mine iniquity, and cleanse me from my sin. 3 For I acknowledge my transgressions: and my sin is ever before me.* That is exactly how I felt. My sin was with me all the time, and I never forgot my failure. *4 Against thee, thee only, have I sinned, and done this evil in thy sight: that thou mightest be justified when thou speakest, and be clear when thou judgest.* That was hard for me, because even though ultimately all sin, even if it harms others, is an offence against God. I am thinking that David failed Bathsheba, Uriah, Joab and everyone else that was involved. While his sin touched and harmed all of them, it was still God who had given him a kingdom and whose love and law David had ignored. *5 Behold, I was shapen in iniquity; and in sin did my mother conceive me. 6 Behold, thou desirest truth in the inward parts: and in the hidden part thou shalt make me to know wisdom. 7 Purge me with hyssop, and I shall be clean: wash me, and I shall be whiter than snow. 8 Make me to hear joy and gladness; that the bones which thou hast broken may rejoice. 9 Hide thy face from my sins, and blot out all mine iniquities.* David says, 'Let the blood of the sacrifice cover my sin; do not focus on what divided us.' David wanted to renew his fellowship with God. David knew that sin was a matter of the heart—an inner problem. The actions he took had come from a place of rebellion within him. *10 Create in me a clean heart, O God; and renew a right spirit within me. 11 Cast me not away from thy presence; and take not thy holy spirit from me. 12 Restore unto me the joy of thy salvation; and uphold me with thy free spirit. 13 Then will I teach transgressors thy ways; and sinners shall be converted unto thee. 14 Deliver me from bloodguiltiness, O God, thou God of my salvation: and my tongue shall sing aloud of thy righteousness. 15 O Lord, open thou my lips; and my mouth shall shew forth thy praise. 16 For thou desirest not sacrifice; else would I give it: thou delightest not in burnt offering. 17 The sacrifices of God are a broken* *spirit: a broken and a contrite heart, O God, thou wilt not despise.* David had walked closely with the Lord. He knew that everything that mattered came from the spirit of man walking in unity with the Lord who made him and loved him. The good news is that the Lord forgave and greatly blessed David and Bathsheba. The next son she bore was Solomon and we all know how much God loved and used him.

Bathsheba and I are like every other woman down through time caught in sexual failure and thrown at the feet of Jesus to be judged and to die in their sin. It was while I was carrying the child no one but me accepted or wanted that I first heard the good news that I could be saved. I prayed with a TV evangelist, but my decision was weak and my knowledge and faith were nonexistent so I cannot really say I was saved, but I opened the door a crack. No stones fell upon me when I did. God was not mad at me after all. There was no noticeable change, except that maybe I was more open to forgiveness. I knew my sin. I loved my child, but I knew shame as well. I did not want anyone looking down on me, I was not proud that I was carrying a child conceived in sin. Most of the time I was at home, and lots of that time I was alone. I dwelt on my failure and the rejection I felt. I had never considered aborting my baby and I could not imagine giving my child up for adoption either. I had lost the man I loved, lost the respect of my parents and my friends, and I had placed my life on a very hard road, but God had a plan to turn it all around.

I met my husband during that time; he became my friend and later I fell in love with him. I married Buzz shortly after Marie was born. She was not his biologically, but he loved us both and our marriage softened the harshness I had lived in. Being loved and married made me feel like my sin was no longer on public display.

I was not really saved for nearly another year, but when I openly admitted my guilt and looked up from my position in the dirt at the feet of Jesus, I saw only love and forgiveness. I heard all the stones of condemnation falling and with every thud, the echo of my Lord. "Neither do I condemn thee: go, and sin no more."

And the Walls Fell Down

Montana is my great-grandson. He is one year old and determined to go where he is not supposed to go. I have gates to trap him in the safe confines of a bedroom and the kitchen and a makeshift wall to keep him in the living room. I have tried to discourage him, but the little guy just wants to explore. He does not know how dangerous the stairs can be and how much I love him and want him safe. All he sees is a wall to challenge. He goes over, under and around whatever he can, but he cannot get through the gate. It is too strong, too high, too tightly wedged into the door frame. The armies of Israel faced a high wall too—one wall in particular threatened to block their path into their promised land.

Jericho was one of the oldest fortified cities in the world. The children of Israel had been told to go in and take the land. Jericho was standing directly in their path, between the Promise of God and the desert. It was necessary to overcome Jericho in order to enter into the Promised Land and take the rest of what became Israel. Most commentaries and archaeologists agree that it was a strongly defended city, with walls of both stone and mud-bricks. According to the Living Bible Encyclopedia, "This city had been surrounded by a double wall, which encircled the summit of the mound. The inner wall was twelve feet thick and the outer six feet. These walls had been violently destroyed and toppled down the slopes of the mound. Layers of ash and charcoal testified to the burning of the city by its captors." (p. 948-949) If the archeological evidence is true, that was a strong fortress for such early armies to face. They were ill-equipped to take on such a strong city. They had no way in the natural to take down double walls eighteen feet deep that surrounded that city.

God had already spoken to Joshua before he faced this fortress. **Joshua 1:5-9 (KJV).** *5 There shall not any man be able to stand before thee all the days of thy life: as I was with Moses, so I will be with thee: I will not fail thee, nor forsake thee. 6 Be strong and of a good courage: for unto this people shalt thou divide for an inheritance the land, which I sware unto their fathers to give them. 7 Only be thou strong and very courageous, that thou mayest observe to do according to all the law, which Moses my servant commanded thee: turn not from it to the right hand or to the left, that thou mayest prosper whithersoever thou goest. 8 This book of the law shall not depart out of thy mouth; but thou shalt meditate therein day and night, that thou mayest observe to do according to all that is written therein: for then thou shalt make thy way prosperous, and then thou shalt have good success. 9 Have not I commanded thee? Be strong and of a good courage; be not afraid, neither be thou dismayed: for the LORD thy God is with thee whithersoever thou goest.* Joshua could stand in the assurance of those words spoken by the God who cannot lie. Joshua knew he would win the battle. That did not mean he was going to just sit idly by and do nothing. He sought the Lord for direction.

Jericho was a formidable obstacle and the Hebrews needed and received divine intervention in order to capture it. No doubt, there will always be obstacles and barriers to where we want to go and what we want to accomplish in life. This time we are looking at a fortress set up to stop you in your tracks. It is an established blockade, one that was built to keep you out of God's will. If you cannot go over or under, then you have to go through it, you have to find a way to knock it down, brick by brick. Jericho is like every other wall in your life. They too will come tumbling down if you do things God's way. Never forget God has promised to go with you and to give you the victory. **Romans 8:31 (KJV)** *31 What shall we then say to these things? If God be for us, who can be against us?* **Romans 8:37-39 (KJV)** *37 Nay, in all these things we are more than conquerors through him that loved us. 38 For I am persuaded, that neither death, nor life, nor angels, nor principalities, nor powers, nor things present, nor things to come, 39 Nor height, nor depth, nor any other creature, shall be able to separate us from the love of God, which is in Christ Jesus our Lord.* That sounds like certain victory to me. We have a closer relationship to the Lord than Joshua ever had. He obeyed and found faith to trust in God until the victory came and every trace of that wall fell down. Our faith has to rise up like that too.

Joshua 6:1-5 (KJV) *1 Now Jericho was straitly shut up because of the children of Israel: none went out, and none came in. 2 And the LORD said unto Joshua, See, I have given into thine hand Jericho, and the king thereof, and the mighty men of valour. 3 And ye shall compass the city, all ye men of war, and go round about the city once. Thus shalt thou do six days. 4 And seven priests shall bear before the ark seven trumpets of rams' horns: and the seventh day ye shall compass the city seven times, and the priests shall blow with the trumpets. 5 And it shall come to pass, that when they make a long blast with the ram's horn, and when ye hear the sound of the trumpet, all the people shall shout with a great shout; and the wall of the city shall fall down flat, and the people shall ascend up every man straight before him.*

How strange the plan of God sounds. They were not told to build a ramp to go over. There was no mention of battering down the gates. They were not even to starve out the inhabitants or set fire to the gates, all being normal ways to attack a walled city. The plan God gave them was to march around the city, then go back to camp. This strategy was way out of the norm. They were to keep their mouths shut. The priests were to carry the Ark of the Covenant, a symbol of God's presence, which weighed between 183 pounds and 288 pounds according to internet sources. That army was thousands strong, and they were told to march around the city, once each day, and then go back to camp, for six days. Then on the seventh day, keep marching in circles around that city and on the seventh time blow the ram's horn in victory. You won't even touch the walls before they fall down flat. Then the men distributed on all sides of the city will enter at once and destroy all that is inside. The inner warriors chafed at the slow progress. As usual, the sceptics wondered at the possibility of anything happening. The believers agreed that whatever God said would work. Joshua was in charge so they did what they were told.

Joshua 6:11-16 (KJV) *11 So the ark of the LORD compassed the city, going about it once: and they came into the camp, and lodged in the camp. 12 And Joshua rose early in the morning, and the priests took up the ark of the LORD. 13 And seven priests bearing seven trumpets of rams' horns before the ark of the LORD went on continually, and blew with the trumpets: and the armed men went before them; but the rereward came after the ark of the LORD, the priests going on, and blowing with the trumpets. 14 And the second day they compassed the city once, and returned into the camp: so they did six days.* Have you ever wondered what the people in Jericho thought? I have. There they are ready for an attack and the army leaves, not once but six days in a row. They are either thinking the Hebrews must be cowards or that the weirdest possible army opposes them. Remember these soldiers saw the Jordan dry up so the Hebrews could cross on dry ground, and they have heard rumors of other miracles that God has done for them. They may be in mortal fear by now. Terror has a way of eating away at people. They could be dreading the next day's march; they don't know it is a seven day timetable. That seventh day, they think it is the same as every day this past week until the Hebrews don't leave. *15 And it came to pass on the seventh day, that they rose early about the dawning of the day, and compassed the city after the same manner seven times: only on that day they compassed the city seven times. 16 And it came to pass at the seventh time, when the priests blew with the trumpets, Joshua said unto the people, Shout; for the LORD hath given you the city.*

Some historians indicated that the walls did not so much "tip over" as to be pressed down vertically into the ground as if the hand of God just pushed them there. I am not sure it matters how they fell, just that they did. Josephus, the historian, recorded it this way. "When they had gone round it seven times, and had stood still a little, the wall fell down, while no instrument of war, nor any other force, was applied to it by the Hebrews." (Josephus p. 128)

Joshua 6:20-21 (KJV) *20 So the people shouted when the priests blew with the trumpets: and it came to pass, when the people heard the sound of the trumpet, and the people shouted with a great shout, that the wall fell down flat, so that the people went up into the city, every man straight before him, and they took the city. 21 And they utterly destroyed all that was in the city, both man and woman, young and old, and ox, and sheep, and ass, with the edge of the sword.*

If you have little ones like Montana in your home, you may have watched the Veggie Tales version of the story, "Josh and the Big Wall." I like it because all the time they march around the city the residents are mocking them… "Keep walking but you won't knock down our wall—keep walking but she isn't gonna fall! It's plain to see, your brains are very small…to think walking will be knocking down our wall." On that seventh day when the horns blow and the entire army shouts, one tiny brick just pops out of place. The guards on top of the wall look startled as that one stone hits the ground. Then the whole wall crumbles and tumbles to the ground. I wonder what Joshua and his army thought as they heard the stones falling? Maybe they were thinking about the mighty God who had promised them victory. If they did believe it, their confidence had to soar. God had a plan for the Hebrews to conquer the whole of the Promised Land. Once they obeyed nothing could keep them from victory.

Jeremiah 29:11 (NIV) *11 For I know the plans I have for you, declares the LORD, plans to prosper you and not to harm you, plans to give you hope and a future.* I know this much, when the enemy puts up a strong wall to block you from your destiny, you have to hear from God and you have to obey God to get to the other side. You might have to fight your way through. You may have to patiently wait until God says to go. And sometimes you may have to do something way out of your comfort zone and out of the norm to get the job done. I know this too, God is faithful and He has a plan to make you successful. So just listen for instructions and obey, and before long that wall that was in front of you will become a small heap of gravel, that you can easily step over or sweep aside.

Stones from the Past

Living in your past can control your future…you must never let your past steal from you. The past will try to build stone walls around us to keep us from the purpose God has ordained for our future. Experience can be a harsh teacher and repeated offences deepen our sense of loss and hurt until they seem insurmountable. Stacking one harsh, hardened, hurtful memory and offence on top of another makes the walls loom high around us until we can see no way out.

There was a young man in the Bible who indeed had a past full of offences to be reckoned with. His name was Joseph. He was the favorite son in a family of twelve sons. His father openly favored him and lavished attention and gifts on him. Joseph also had a special anointing in his life, and the Lord gave him prophetic dreams. In the foolishness of his youth, Joseph boasted of the dreams God had given him. He boasted that his brothers all bowed down to him in his dream and the jealousy and hatred in his brothers burned hot against him. His father spent more time with Joseph than his brothers; sometimes they were off working while he was at home leisurely hearing all that God had taught Jacob. He is the son of Jacob's favorite wife, Rachel and since her death the boy has become spoiled. Jacob even gave him a coat of many colors. "It was a coat that represented 'favor', which by right probably belonged to the first born, Reuben, but it was given to Joseph." (Edmond, p. 27) One day when his brothers were in the fields with the sheep, seventeen year old Joseph was sent to check on their wellbeing and return to his father. So Joseph goes off, inappropriately wearing that coat which was a source of irritation and conflict, to search for his brothers. They consider him their rival, and a tattle tale, they are fed up with Joseph.

Genesis 37:18-28 (KJV) *18 And when they saw him afar off, even before he came near unto them, they conspired against him to slay him. 19 And they said one to another, Behold, this dreamer cometh. 20 Come now therefore, and let us slay him, and cast him into some pit, and we will say, Some evil beast hath devoured him: and we shall see what will become of his dreams. 21 And Reuben heard it, and he delivered him out of their hands; and said, Let us not kill him. 22 And Reuben said unto them, Shed no blood, but cast him into this pit that is in the wilderness, and lay no hand upon him; that he might rid him out of their hands, to deliver him to his father again. 23 And it came to pass, when Joseph was come unto his brethren, that they stript Joseph out of his coat, his coat of many colours that was on him; 24 And they took him, and cast him into a pit: and the pit was empty, there was no water in it.* Their jealousy became hatred and in the end they were willing to let him starve to death. They could hear him crying out for help, pleading with them to pull him out of the pit, while they sat feasting just a few feet away. *25 And they sat down to eat bread: and they lifted up their eyes and looked, and, behold, a company of Ishmeelites came from Gilead with their camels bearing spicery and balm and myrrh, going to carry it down to Egypt. 26 And Judah said unto his brethren, What profit is it if we slay our brother, and conceal his blood? 27 Come, and let us sell him to the Ishmeelites, and let not our hand be upon him; for he is our brother and our flesh. And his brethren were content.* He says, 'I don't want to feel guilty for killing him, but I want him gone and we can make some money off of his misery.' *28 Then there passed by Midianites merchantmen; and they drew and lifted up Joseph out of the pit, and sold Joseph to the Ishmeelites for* *twenty pieces of silver: and they brought Joseph into Egypt.* Joseph leaves home a contented but spoiled teenager. Then his brothers capture him and throw him into a pit, or cistern, planning to let him die slowly of starvation and exposure. Finally, they get the bright idea to sell him into slavery. They take money to be rid of him and they enjoy the fact that he will be treated harshly and unfairly. "Joseph was a victim of human trafficking." (Edmond, p. 28) At that point he could have entered into a deep state of self-pity, and a mountain of resentment could have fortified the wrongs done to him. There are people who have endured much less who take on a victim mentality, and live in constant offence.

Joseph was probably shackled and dragged through the desert. After walking for miles day after day, he and the traders arrive in Egypt. He is to be sold as a slave, so more than likely he is stripped naked and standing on an auction block in the middle of town so people can bid on him. He could have become very bitter. He could have held great anger and hatred in his heart against his brothers and his captors and then against the man who purchased him to work as a slave, but according to what is written in the Scriptures, he did not. "As horrible as all of this looks, Joseph had begun his journey that would take him to the fulfillment of his purpose and destiny. Your destiny is bigger than your circumstances." (Edmond, p. 29) It is easy to say that after the fact, but during the trial, it is almost impossible to see how God could have orchestrated his situation.

Genesis 39:1-6 (KJV) *1 And Joseph was brought down to Egypt; and Potiphar, an officer of Pharaoh, captain of the guard, an Egyptian, bought him of the hands of the Ishmeelites, which had brought him down thither. 2 And the LORD was with Joseph, and he was a prosperous man; and he was in the house of his master the Egyptian. 3 And his master saw that the LORD was with him, and that the LORD made all that he did to prosper in his hand. 4 And Joseph found grace in his sight, and he served him: and he made him overseer over his house, and all that he had he put into his hand. 5 And it came to pass from the time that he had made him overseer in his house, and over all that he had, that the LORD blessed the*

Egyptian's house for Joseph's sake; and the blessing of the LORD was upon all that he had in the house, and in the field. 6 And he left all that he had in Joseph's hand; and he knew not ought he had, save the bread which he did eat. And Joseph was a goodly person, and well favoured. Joseph has maintained his integrity and the Lord is using him and blessing him even while in slavery. He has improved his conditions by being faithful and receives a measure of freedom and authority because of it. He faithfully served Potiphar for at least eleven years.

Not to let the story end here, one day his owner's wife became intrigued by this young Hebrew slave. She watches him and her lust burns toward him. The insinuation is that she has been unfaithful before and it is not a big deal to her to throw herself shamelessly at this handsome young man who is in her household. She flirts and taunts and propositions Joseph day after day, but he refuses her advances. It would be a violation of Potiphar's trust to do as she suggested, and it would also be a sin because he knew her to be another man's wife. For Joseph, sinning against God was too terrible to imagine, and so he avoided her as much as he could.

Genesis 39:7-12 (KJV) *7 And it came to pass after these things, that his master's wife cast her eyes upon Joseph; and she said, Lie with me. 8 But he refused, and said unto his master's wife, Behold, my master wotteth not what is with me in the house, and he hath committed all that he hath to my hand; 9 There is none greater in this house than I; neither hath he kept back any thing from me but thee, because thou art his wife: how then can I do this great wickedness, and sin against God? 10 And it came to pass, as she spake to Joseph day by day, that he hearkened not unto her, to lie by her, or to be with her. 11 And it came to pass about this time, that Joseph went into the house to do his business; and there was none of the men of the house there within. 12 And she caught him by his garment, saying, Lie with me: and he left his garment in her hand, and fled, and got him out.* He ran from temptation, but her grip was so tight upon him that she tore off his outer tunic.

Genesis 39:13-20 (KJV) *13 And it came to pass, when she saw that he had left his garment in her hand, and was fled forth, 14 That she called unto the men of her house, and spake unto them, saying, See, he hath brought in an Hebrew unto us to mock us; he came in unto me to lie with me, and I cried with a loud voice:* She used their prejudice to make her story seem more believable. *15 And it came to pass, when he heard that I lifted up my voice and cried, that he left his garment with me, and fled, and got him out. 16 And she laid up his garment by her, until his lord came home. 17 And she spake unto him according to these words, saying, The Hebrew servant, which thou hast brought unto us, came in unto me to mock me: 18 And it came to pass, as I lifted up my voice and cried, that he left his garment with me, and fled out. 19 And it came to pass, when his master heard the words of his wife, which she spake unto him, saying, After this manner did thy servant to me; that his wrath was kindled. 20 And Joseph's master took him, and put him into the prison, a place where the king's prisoners were bound: and he was there in the prison.* If Potiphar really believed that Joseph had attempted to rape his wife, he would have had him killed. He must have suspected that things were not entirely as she reported, but in order to maintain a pretense of power and authority, and to offer some honor to his wife, he throws Joseph into prison.

There in the dark stone dungeon, Joseph has time to think. He could add this as another offence to his list of insults and injuries and reasons to be angry and bitter. If he did that the prison around him would have gotten inside him. "He was framed, but his attitude didn't change. He was there to be a blessing and serve a purpose. As a result, each thing that he encountered elevated him. Every obstacle simply became a stepping stone. The difference between a stepping stone and a stumbling stone is how high you lift your feet. His attitude facilitated the blessing and gave him the green light from God to move to the next level." (Edmond, p. 33) He chose to accept his fate and serve well where he was. Even during his years in prison, God's hand was upon him for promotion. **Genesis 39:21-23 (KJV)** *21 But the LORD was with Joseph, and shewed him mercy, and gave him favour in the sight of the keeper of the prison. 22 And* *the keeper of the prison committed to Joseph's hand all the prisoners that were in the prison; and whatsoever they did there, he was the doer of it. 23 The keeper of the prison looked not to any thing that was under his hand; because the LORD was with him, and that which he did, the LORD made it to prosper.*

While in prison, Joseph remained faithful to God and served the warden and other prisoners well. He distinguished himself as an honorable man. He even interpreted dreams for other prisoners. One of them promised to speak to Pharaoh and mention the injustice done to Joseph. For months, he waited, but no word was spoken, and Joseph still lay in prison. I am sure that seemed like an unnecessary and unhappy delay, but God has perfect timing for His plans and it was not time for Joseph's final promotion. Most people don't realize that it was at least nineteen long years that Joseph spent in the pit and slavery and the prison and in all those years he never grew bitter. Some would say he had a right to be angry but it was not going to benefit him to carry a grudge. At the end of two full years, when Pharaoh had a dream, Joseph was finally remembered. He is called to interpret the dream and having insight that came from God, he gave wise council to Pharaoh. Joseph is immediately elevated to the highest position in the land of Egypt. He has authority over all of Egypt's resources and all of the people. Joseph controls storehouses full of riches. It is interesting that he did not use his position to seek out revenge or even a reunion with his estranged brothers. He simply served faithfully for another seven years of prosperity, and the first two years of famine. He was faithful where he was until God again intervened in his circumstances.

When the predicted famine covers the earth, Joseph's brothers come to him seeking food. They did not recognize this middle-aged Joseph, who was dressed like and speaks like an Egyptian. He did not react with harsh words of condemnation; in fact, Joseph saw a higher purpose in what happened to him. He sells them grain and eventually reveals himself to them. **Genesis 42:6-8 (KJV)** *6 And Joseph was the governor over the land, and he it was that sold to all the people of the land: and Joseph's brethren came, and bowed down* *themselves before him with their faces to the earth.* He has seen his vision fulfilled. *7 And Joseph saw his brethren, and he knew them, but made himself strange unto them, and spake roughly unto them; and he said unto them, Whence come ye? And they said, From the land of Canaan to buy food. 8 And Joseph knew his brethren, but they knew not him.* …**Genesis 45:1-7 (KJV)** *1 Then Joseph could not refrain himself before all them that stood by him; and he cried, Cause every man to go out from me. And there stood no man with him, while Joseph made himself known unto his brethren. 2 And he wept aloud: and the Egyptians and the house of Pharaoh heard. 3 And Joseph said unto his brethren, I am Joseph; doth my father yet live? And his brethren could not answer him; for they were troubled at his presence. 4 And Joseph said unto his brethren, Come near to me, I pray you. And they came near. And he said, I am Joseph your brother, whom ye sold into Egypt. 5 Now therefore be not grieved, nor angry with yourselves, that ye sold me hither: for God did send me before you to preserve life. 6 For these two years hath the famine been in the land: and yet there are five years, in the which there shall neither be earing nor harvest. 7 And God sent me before you to preserve you a posterity in the earth, and to save your lives by a great deliverance.* Joseph saw the big picture, if God had not allowed him to be enslaved in Egypt; his entire family would have starved. He said, maybe you meant to harm me but God has used it to save all of us. His words remind me of what Paul wrote to the church in Rome. **Romans 8: 28 (KJV)** *28 And we know that all things work together for good to them that love God, to them who are the called according to his purpose.* He recognized that the plan of God took him through the pit and the prison to the palace for a purpose. Nothing that happened to him was by accident and none of it was wasted. "Your response to your circumstances is not about your circumstances. It is about your belief and trust." (Edmund, p. 77)

Joseph could have focused on all the wrong done to him, and become bitter. He chose not to do that; he did not let his past damage his future. He had gone from pampered to the pit—he had been favored and hated. Joseph had been in prison, but now he is in the palace and he understands that every step along the way positioned him to save his family, and he has a heart to forgive. He made the stones of possible offence into stepping stones to get out of bondage. "These past experiences, if not faced, will continue to be daily experiences. Forgiveness is not just a once-in-a-while thing; it must be a way of life. It is a life-style that will be a happy, secure one." (Hicks, p. 80) That is what Joseph had done. Day by day, throughout the years of suffering and bondage he had walked in integrity and in forgiveness. Not once in all those years did he curse his brothers or wallow in the mire of self-pity.

Offences will come, but you don't have to take offence. So many times I've had someone say to me, "I'm sorry about such and such." Most of the time, I have no idea what they are talking about. I just refuse to take offence. I never let a supposed wrong or an irrational thought about others take me hostage. Our pastor taught us that when we are offended we are basically useless to God, so I refuse to stay bound up by the words or actions of others. I try to think and act like Joseph, who did not allow the circumstances around him to imprison him.

Our past does not have to harden us and barricade us behind the walls of bitterness, insecurity and regret. We choose how we respond to the things that come our way. Joseph could not control everything that happened to him, but what he could do is react in a godly manner. He could separate the God who loved him from the troubles that befell him. You can do the same thing. "I refuse to let my mouth violate my believing heart by uttering anything that defeats the finished work of my Lord Jesus on the cross for me. My insecurities fade away as I realize my security in Christ." (Hicks, p. 48)

I have a dear friend who once struggled with her teenage daughter. We will call my friend Ann and her daughter Emma, because I would never want to reveal their real names and risk embarrassing either of them. When Emma was young, she went to church and professed Christ. Off and on she seemed to really love the Lord. When she was a teenager she became distant and secretive. Ann was frustrated because Emma had fallen in with the wrong crowd. Her grades were slipping, and she was angry all the time. Frequently, Ann responded in anger too. One day Ann found a discarded pregnancy test in the trash. There was drinking and maybe drugs. Ann suspected it but was not sure. The devil was building a wall between her and her daughter that seemed impossible to tear down. The years went by and the damage became worse every day. A towering wall of emotional stones loomed between them. The devil was stacking them up one offence at a time. They were both imprisoned by the wall and could not reach each other.

One night when all seemed lost and the distance between mother and daughter was great, Ann had a dream. She told the dream something like this. "I was crying so hard; I was beaten and bloodied and was bound by a rope. I was laying on the railroad tracks. It was like the old movies when the villain leaves you there to die. I was struggling against the ropes when I first heard the whistle of a train. I was praying 'Oh Jesus help me.' I looked into the distance and there it was—a huge locomotive with smoke billowing from the stacks. When the train came into focus, I could see a platform full of kids on top. They were drinking and laughing. Someone pointed to the tracks where I was held captive and I saw Emma look at me and laugh before turning aside to kiss her boyfriend. It was as if she knew I was about to die and she didn't care.

I was still crying and praying and the train kept barreling closer and closer. Finally, I lost hope of being saved and I no longer prayed for my freedom. I was praying only for Emma who was so deceived. The train kept coming and I was sure I would die. Then I saw something change on Emma's face and even though the train was loud now, I could hear her shouting, "No, I don't want my mom to die, I want my family back…stop, I'm sorry—I change my mind, please stop." Then I saw Jesus running from the other direction and I thought He would release me in time to save me from the crushing wheels that drew near. But when He got near the train, He turned away from me. He wasn't coming to untie me or lift me from the rails. He did not appear to be stopping the train either, or even lifting Emma from it. He ran past the teenagers on the platform car, past dozens of rail cars, and past the caboose. It looked like He was running away from us. When Jesus was behind the train, He picked up the tracks and shook them like you would shake a dusty rug. Everything on the tracks came off, the people and the train flew through the air, but I did not see destruction and death. All I saw was Emma walking toward me with tears in her eyes. Later I asked Jesus, "Why didn't you just save me or Emma?" This is what the Lord said to me. "I had to go back into her past to root up all the things that put Emma on that train. I had to take out all of the hurt between you and the sins that you both committed along the way. I had to remove the guilt and anger and sorrow so you could be a family again."

Emma did not change right after the dream. It was years of struggle. Eventually, Emma moved out of the house to live with her boyfriend. The walls grew stronger and the silence was deafening. Ann held to the promise of God in that dream. When the days were hard, she remembered the words Jesus spoke to her, and thanked God that Jesus was running toward the tracks. Emma bore a child out of wedlock and the love for that baby helped to open the door to restoration. Today, Emma has moved back home. Things aren't perfect, but they are better. Ann and I rejoiced that the Lord broke down the walls between them, rooted out all the past so they could begin again. That first day when Emma sat and talked with her mom, she heard the sound of a rock falling from the wall. There are still a few stones on the ground between them, but God will finish what He has begun.

Joel 2:28-29 (KJV) *28 And it shall come to pass afterward, that I will pour out my spirit upon all flesh; and your sons and your daughters shall prophesy, your old men shall dream dreams, your young men shall see visions: 29 And also upon the servants and upon the handmaids in those days will I pour out my spirit.* Ann was one of those whose message came as an inspired dream.

Most of us get stuck because we can't see the love of God and the love for or from others. We have a deep longing for more. We hunger after that strong relationship. Most of us are seeking a love that satisfies in all kinds of places. But the One who made us loves us perfectly. If we will let Him, He will fill us from the inside out. It is only when we let God in that our other relationships seem to work out.

He gave Ann the dream to build her hope, so she could see past the walls that divided her from her daughter. He is also the same God who gave Joseph a dream of his brothers bowing down to him, which they did. Joseph's attitude, his actions and his obedience saved all of Israel. He walked in integrity and because He did the linage of Christ was preserved.

When in bondage, it is best to hold to the promise of God and rest knowing that He will restore hope and love. Only God can go into your past and remove the hurt of it. Only God can break down the barriers that are there. He is willing to do just that for you.

Luke 22:32(KJV) *32 But I have prayed for thee, that thy faith fail not: and when thou art converted, strengthen thy brethren.*

Living In the Rubble

Peter denied Christ, and his failure as a friend and disciple had to have caused him great anguish. He could have stayed in that place of condemnation and wallowed in the rubble of his past failure, but he would have never reached his potential. He had to tear down the walls of shame and regret and clean away all the rubble that blocked his path. It was a lot to forget, a lot to repent of, but Peter had to get past his mistake—past his sin or he would be forever held prisoner in it.

It is Passover and the disciples are sitting together enjoying a good meal. **Matthew 26:31-35 (KJV)** *31 Then saith Jesus unto them, All ye shall be offended because of me this night: for it is written, I will smite the shepherd, and the sheep of the flock shall be scattered abroad. 32 But after I am risen again, I will go before you into Galilee. 33 Peter answered and said unto him, Though all men shall be offended because of thee, yet will I never be offended. 34 Jesus said unto him, Verily I say unto thee, That this night, before the cock crow, thou shalt deny me thrice. 35 Peter said unto him, Though I should die with thee, yet will I not deny thee. Likewise also said all the disciples.*

Peter is bold. After all, he has seen the power of the Messiah as Jesus raised the dead, and healed the sick. He even walked on the water with Jesus. He knows this is the Christ and he vows to stand with Jesus against all enemies. 'If everyone else deserts you, I will stand by you; I am willing to die for you.' These are the bold words of one resting quietly in a place of safety. Like us, Peter thinks he stands firm. He knows Jesus. He says, 'I'm solid,' but the pressure was about to come and he would fail.

Luke 22:31-34 (KJV) *31 And the Lord said, Simon, Simon, behold, Satan hath desired to have you, that he may sift you as wheat: 32 But I have prayed for thee, that thy faith fail not: and when thou art converted, strengthen thy brethren.* The same Lord who said you will deny me three times also says after you have repented, you will help others. Jesus knew that Peter would climb out of despair and honestly repent. He knew Peter would not wallow in the rubble of his failure for long. *33 And he said unto him, Lord, I am ready to go with thee, both into prison, and to death. 34 And he said, I tell thee, Peter, the cock shall not crow this day, before that thou shalt thrice deny that thou knowest me.*

Peter could not see himself denying the Master, but he would indeed do exactly that. I am sure he was troubled as he considered those words, on the walk toward Gethsemane. **Matthew 26:36-41 (KJV)** *36 Then cometh Jesus with them unto a place called Gethsemane, and saith unto the disciples, Sit ye here, while I go and pray yonder.* It is a familiar place, where they rested and prayed habitually there is nothing that makes this time different in Peter's heart. So Jesus takes His closest friends, His inner circle of disciples, Peter, James and John and He says *'Watch and pray.'* Jesus longs for their support as He struggles against the enormity of the world's sin. Jesus has to embrace the fullness of all sin and the judgment to come. They could not have understood the spiritual battle taking place just a few feet away. While He begins to take within himself all the vile stain of centuries full of sin, and stares natural and spiritual death in the face, they nod off. *40 And he cometh unto the disciples, and findeth them asleep, and saith unto Peter, What, could* *ye not watch with me one hour?* 'I will die for you but don't expect me to stay awake and pray.' Jesus tells him: *41 Watch and pray, that ye enter not into temptation: the spirit indeed is willing, but the flesh is weak.* Three times Jesus goes and makes covenant with the Father and sweats great drops of blood, and each time He returns to His most faithful followers, to find them resting. They are unaware of the gravity of the moment until a great crowd comes to arrest Jesus. These were the very men Jesus entrusted with the message of Salvation. If these men failed to preach and teach and testify of the resurrection there would be no fruit from His great sacrifice. Peter and these others would be called upon to risk their lives to nurture the early church, and they cannot even give up a little sleep for Him. That memory alone could have buried them in an avalanche of guilt.

The scripture tells us that Judas betrayed Him and that a great crowd of men came with swords and clubs to arrest Jesus. Peter drew a sword as if to fight off those taking his master. The Scripture also says, **Matthew 26:56 (KJV)** *56 Then all the disciples forsook him, and fled.* By their actions all of the disciples failed Him; their fear and flight denied their relationship to Him. Most of the disciples just ran into the night, but Peter secretly followed at a distance, hiding in the shadows. When Jesus is taken before the Sanhedrin to be tried, Peter is in the courtyard.

No one boldly went with Jesus as He was dragged before the Sanhedrin. **Matthew 26:58 (KJV)** *58 But Peter followed him afar off unto the high priest's palace, and went in, and sat with the servants, to see the end.* Peter hung out just a short physical distance from the Lord and warmed himself by the enemy's fire. He took an interest in what the outcome would be but did not put himself in too much danger. He had a fearful wait and see attitude. The man of commitment seems missing. The man of action from the garden has cowered. Every compromise pulls him farther into the shadows and he is now standing in the court of the enemy, undetected, his very presence there feels like a betrayal against the Lord.

When Peter is confronted by a young girl with no real status or power, he denies knowing Jesus. Then someone else sees him and says, 'Weren't you there in the garden?' Peter denies it again with more emphasis. Finally, the men press in around him. They are beginning to draw attention to him, and there is some real danger. Peter denies the Lord again, cursing and swearing and then the rooster crows. Fear captured him and then horrible sorrow followed. **Matthew 26:75 (KJV)** *75 And Peter remembered the word of Jesus, which said unto him, Before the cock crow, thou shalt deny me thrice. And he went out, and wept bitterly.*

Peter didn't have to follow from far off. It might have been better for him if he had just run away like the other disciples did. They had all been cowards, but they did not have to live with what he spoke, the vocal denial. They had not lied about their allegiance. The author of Luke added one additional comment to his account. **Luke 22:61-62 (KJV)** *61 And the Lord turned, and looked upon Peter. And Peter remembered the word of the Lord, how he had said unto him, Before the cock crow, thou shalt deny me thrice. 62 And Peter went out, and wept bitterly.* Jesus looked at him. How hard that compassionate, knowing look would have been to take. Shame and remorse rained down upon Peter. It was probably easier for the other disciples to repent, than it was for Peter.

Like Peter, we don't intend to fail the Lord. Somehow we ease into sin. Maybe we get too comfortable in His presence and we lose that sense of awe. There was a time that the disciples said, *"Who is this man that even the wind and sea obey him."* Now they don't even draw near so He can feel their support in His darkest hour. They had seen the sick healed and watched Him provide for the hungry multitudes. They had first-hand knowledge of His teachings, His unshakable love, and His compassion and so do we. Like them we are grateful but distanced at heart and following from a place apart. We, like Peter, are getting too much in the flesh and warming ourselves in the comfort of the nearest fire—casual in our faith until we nearly deny Him ourselves.

After the Lord was crucified, the disciples felt like all their hopes were buried with Him in the tomb. I think of Peter, how he denied the Lord three times and each time with more emphasis, more anger, finally even cursing. How hopeless he must have felt. Peter, more than any of the disciples must have felt he had sinned so deeply that he had nullified his place in the ministry. God still had plans for Peter; He would not leave him in his deep despair. He was specifically singled out to see the resurrected Christ. **Mark 16:5-7 (KJV)** *5 And entering into the sepulchre, they saw a young man sitting on the right side, clothed in a long white garment; and they were affrighted. 6 And he saith unto them, Be not affrighted: Ye seek Jesus of Nazareth, which was crucified: he is risen; he is not here: behold the place where they laid him. 7 But go your way, <u>tell his disciples and Peter</u> that he goeth before you into Galilee: there shall ye see him, as he said unto you.* I love it that the angel told Mary to 'Tell the disciples and Peter, I will meet them.' He instructed her specifically, 'Make sure you tell Peter.' God wanted him restored. If the angel had not called him by name, maybe Peter would have thought there was no hope for him. Maybe he would have imagined that the Lord would not forgive his denial. His regret could have become a stronger tomb than the one Jesus had lain in.

All of the disciples went to meet with the Lord in Galilee. When Jesus showed up on shore, He gave Peter three opportunities to repent and he took them all. **John 21:15-19 (KJV)** *15 So when they had dined, Jesus saith to Simon Peter...* The name Simon meant one that wavers, a reed blown by the wind. After all, we have seen instability in his character. However, the name Peter meant a rock, steadfast and sure. The Lord used both names, because Peter got to choose his future. He could stay stuck in the past with his failure ever before him, or he could stand up as a strong leader and go forth in the power of the resurrection and live out his destiny. *Jesus saith to Simon Peter, Simon, son of Jonas, lovest thou me more than these? He saith unto him, Yea, Lord; thou knowest that I love thee. He saith unto him, Feed my lambs. 16 He saith to him again the second time, Simon, son of Jonas, lovest thou me? He saith unto him, Yea, Lord; thou knowest that I love thee. He saith unto him,*

Feed my sheep. 17 He saith unto him the third time, Simon, son of Jonas, lovest thou me? Peter was grieved because he said unto him the third time, Lovest thou me? And he said unto him, Lord, thou knowest all things; thou knowest that I love thee. Jesus saith unto him, Feed my sheep... And when he had spoken this, he saith unto him, Follow me. Do you love me? 'Yes Lord, I do love you.' He said it once for every time he denied his Lord. Then God made of him a solid rock of a disciple who called thousands to repentance and won souls to the Lord of all prodigals. Peter knocked down every wall of remorse, guilt and shame with those words "I love you." Those words brought him freedom as the rocks came tumbling down. I am sure that sometimes the memory of his denial resurfaced but each time Peter just kicked away the debris, and walked on in confident assurance that the Lord had forgiven him.

Romans 8:35 (KJV) *35 Who shall separate us from the love of Christ? shall tribulation, or distress, or persecution, or famine, or nakedness, or peril, or sword?* No, they are not enough and neither is our guilt, failure or shame. **Romans 8:38-39 (KJV)** *38 For I am persuaded, that neither death, nor life, nor angels, nor principalities, nor powers, nor things present, nor things to come, 39 Nor height, nor depth, nor any other creature, shall be able to separate us from the love of God, which is in Christ Jesus our Lord.* We have to purposefully, choose to walk with Him daily. We have to go forward, unhindered by the remnants of our past failures.

Remember when the city of Jerusalem was taken captive and the walls and gates destroyed. One man with a vision believed, 'We can rebuild it.' Nehemiah motived the community to start afresh, but first they had to decide that this was not the way they wanted to live. They had to see the potential of a renewed life inside those currently broken city walls. The people wanted a better life, but they also became tired and discouraged. Every trace of past failure and regret has the potential to block our goals. When God had them rebuild the city of Jerusalem, they used burned bricks, burned stones, and damaged materials. If God could use that stuff to rebuild a natural place and fill it with His glory, He can also use you and all your brokenness. "Today, when you go to buy stones or bricks for a building the most expensive ones you can buy are those that have been used. The burned bricks make the most beautiful walls and fireplaces because they show a contrast. Not one is alike. God uses your past because there are certain people whom only you can reach. (Hickey, p.18) When people see who you used to be and who you are now that you are saved, they see that contrast and it points to God. "God uses that contrast as a witness and to help you rebuild the walls of other people's personalities. (Hickey, p.18)

Nehemiah 4:10 (NIV) *10 Meanwhile, the people in Judah said, "The strength of the laborers is giving out, and there is so much rubble that we cannot rebuild the wall."* The devil wants us to just give up. They almost collapsed under the weight of the work, and then they found the strength to remove the debris and rubbish and take all those bits of stone and start over. They figured out that there were some things that just amounted to trash and they threw them away. Then they salvaged what was useful to build with. They worked to make their lives count and their actions successful. That is what Peter did and what we have to do as well. Peter, who openly denied the Lord in the courtyard, also boldly said I love you on the shores of Galilee. There is healing and forgiveness for past mistakes. Somehow we have to see ourselves outside of the prison of our past failure and stand up to say, I am ready to move on. We find a way to look at what is just rubbish from that time and toss it out. We pick up what is still useful to the Lord and see that He can make something beautiful with our damaged past.

Deuteronomy 30:19 (KJV) *19 I call heaven and earth to record this day against you, that I have set before you life and death, blessing and cursing: therefore choose life, that both thou and thy seed may live:* It is always our choice. Most of the time, we are the last to forgive ourselves. Even when God has forgiven, and people have long forgotten, we sometimes hold on to our failures. We have to drop those rocks and press on, leaving the place where we messed up. We have to purposefully turn away from the past, leaving our sin, not letting it hold us captive any longer.

Peter never denied Jesus again. It was Peter who led the early church. It was Peter who preached at Pentecost and saw 3000 saved. When the first miracles occurred they were at the command of this man who had previously denied even knowing Christ. **Acts 3:5-8 (KJV)** *5 And he gave heed unto them, expecting to receive something of them. 6 Then Peter said, Silver and gold have I none; but such as I have give I thee: In the name of Jesus Christ of Nazareth rise up and walk. 7 And he took him by the right hand, and lifted him up: and immediately his feet and ankle bones received strength. 8 And he leaping up stood, and walked, and entered with them into the temple, walking, and leaping, and praising God.* Although, Peter was arrested and challenged, just look at the boldness that he displayed. **Acts 4:7-13 (KJV)** *7 And when they had set them in the midst, they asked, By what power, or by what name, have ye done this? 8 Then Peter, filled with the Holy Ghost, said unto them, Ye rulers of the people, and elders of Israel, 9 If we this day be examined of the good deed done to the impotent man, by what means he is made whole; 10 Be it known unto you all, and to all the people of Israel, that by the name of Jesus Christ of Nazareth, whom ye crucified, whom God raised from the dead, even by him doth this man stand here before you whole. 11 This is the stone which was set at nought of you builders, which is become the head of the corner. 12 Neither is there salvation in any other: for there is none other name under heaven given among men, whereby we must be saved. 13 Now when they saw the boldness of Peter and John, and perceived that they were unlearned and ignorant men, they marvelled; and they took knowledge of them, that they had been with Jesus.* There is the evidence of a changed man. Peter is not fearful, he is confident. He pressed on, took hold of forgiveness and walked free of the bondage that could have paralyzed him with fear and shame.

If Peter could hear the rocks of that self-imposed mental prison fall to the ground, so can you. Whatever has happened in your life, it is in the past. Let it go. Break out of that place where you have been stuck. Hear the sound of those walls falling down all around you; the prison is crumbling. You still have today and tomorrow to show the world what being with Jesus can do for your life.

Altar Stones

Altars are places of holy sacrifice. In the Old Testament they were always made of uncut stones or mounds of earth. An altar was the place where man would offer blood and incense. It was also the place where God would manifest His approval. The altar was the center of Jewish worship and the essence of the blood covenant.

We know that Able offered a lamb on his altar. God responded by sending fire to consume the sacrifice and show His pleasure in the one who offered it. Noah built an altar when he left the ark, and of course there is that famous altar where Abraham intended to slay Isaac. Altars were an important part of all Old Testament worship. The New International Dictionary of the Bible states that altars were vital to approaching God. They were used not only by the Hebrews but also in pagan religious practices, some of which were heinous and brutal. Any altar to Jehovah was holy. "It was the place of sacrifice where God was propitiated and where man was pardoned and sanctified. It looked to the great sacrifice that the Son of God was about to make on the cross. The altar of sacrifice, the first thing visible as one approached the tabernacle, spoke loudly to man that without the shedding of blood there would be no access to God and no forgiveness of sin [Heb. 9:9, 22]." (Douglas, p. 38)

When Adam sinned, all of mankind was forever changed; his sin was passed down to every generation. Mankind had become spiritually dead, separated from God and doomed to hell. Every one of us was found guilty of sin, judged and pronounced worthy of death. That death sentence was paid, but not by us—it fell upon Jesus our Savior. **Romans 3:23-25 (KJV)** *23 For all have sinned, and come short of the glory of God; 24 Being justified freely by his grace through the redemption that is in Christ Jesus: 25 Whom God hath set forth to be a propitiation [a substitute sacrifice] through faith in his blood, to declare his righteousness for the remission of sins that are past, through the forbearance of God;* He was our representative, our lamb, bearing our sins in His own body on the altar of the cross. **1 Corinthians 15:22 (KJV)** *22 For as in Adam all die, even so in Christ shall all be made alive.* Life and death were in the blood. No man born from Adam's race could possibly be our redeemer. All of mankind was tainted by original sin. No man would ever be good enough to offer anything worthy of redemption. The life of God was in the blood of Jesus and once shed it could be transfused into any fallen being who would allow the sacrifice to become their own. He identified with us, bore the death penalty for us, and we partook of His death and then eternal life. When Jesus died to sin, we all received forgiveness and having passed through death with Him, we were no longer in fear and bondage to it. When He overcame the grave, mankind was resurrected as well.

The reason God redeemed mankind is that God's love was stronger than man's rebellion. **John 3:16-17 (KJV)** *16 For God so loved the world, that he gave his only begotten Son, that whosoever believeth in him should not perish, but have everlasting life. 17 For God sent not his Son into the world to condemn the world; but that the world through him might be saved.* His love motivated and compelled Him to act by sending His Son to buy us out of bondage with a sacrificial offering of His own blood.

Romans 5:8-15 (KJV) *8 But God commendeth his love toward us, in that, while we were yet sinners, Christ died for us. 9 Much more then, being now justified by his blood, we shall be saved from wrath* *through him. 10 For if, when we were enemies, we were reconciled to God by the death of his Son, much more, being reconciled, we shall be saved by his life. 11 And not only so, but we also joy in God through our Lord Jesus Christ, by whom we have now received the atonement. 12 Wherefore, as by one man sin entered into the world, and death by sin; and so death passed upon all men, for that all have sinned... 15 But not as the offence, so also is the free gift. For if through the offence of one many be dead, much more the grace of God, and the gift by grace, which is by one man, Jesus Christ, hath abounded unto many.* Redemption outweighed the sin debt of the entire world. That redemption is freely dispensed to any individual for the asking. There was more than enough holy blood shed there to pay for any sin mankind would ever commit. The blood of Jesus, the righteous Son of God, was poured out for sinners so that man could go free.

Galatians 2:20 (KJV) *20 I am crucified with Christ: nevertheless I live; yet not I, but Christ liveth in me: and the life which I now live in the flesh I live by the faith of the Son of God, who loved me, and gave Himself for me.* The price was paid, the gift was given. Salvation was available to every man. In Christ, the old man of sin died and gave birth to a new life in the old shell. That born again man was infused with the righteousness of God.

Colossians 2:13-15 (KJV) *13 And you, being dead in your sins and the uncircumcision of your flesh, hath he quickened together with him, having forgiven you all trespasses; 14 Blotting out the handwriting of ordinances that was against us, which was contrary to us, and took it out of the way, nailing it to his cross; 15 And having spoiled principalities and powers, he made a shew of them openly, triumphing over them in it.* That is such an amazing picture of what happened on the cross. Long ago there was a custom, that when a man owed a debt that was beyond his ability to pay, he would take the bill, a legal document listing the whole of his debt, and nail it to the front door-post of his home. It was a desperate, humiliating thing to resort to, but when you have more debt than you can ever pay, you do whatever you have to do. The hope was that either the lender or some other wealthy man would show mercy and pay the debt. If a benefactor chose to assume the debt, the payer would fold over the paper hiding the original debt and place his seal upon it showing that it was paid in full. That is exactly what happened at the cross. The accusations, the list of our individual offences and the full weight of our sin debt were written out and Jesus nailed it to the cross, the blood of heaven poured over it, covering it until not a single word could be read. Justice demanded blood; our debt was eternal death, which Jesus willingly paid in full.

Jesus offered the final sacrifice on the cross of Calvary. He paid for our sins, and represented every sinner when He poured out his own blood to buy our redemption. **Ephesians 1:7 (MSG)** 7 *Because of the sacrifice of the Messiah, his blood poured out on the altar of the Cross, we're a free people—free of penalties and punishments chalked up by all our misdeeds. And not just barely free, either. Abundantly free!* Anyone the Son sets free is free indeed.

We put nothing on the altar now but our own will and selfish desires. The final sacrifice was Jesus and when we accepted Him as our personal Savior we were set free from the need to offer up anything to find peace with God. We do not have to be good enough, Jesus was. We do not have to pay the price because He did. **Hebrews 9:24-28 (NIV)** *24 For Christ did not enter a sanctuary made with human hands that was only a copy of the true one; he entered heaven itself, now to appear for us in God's presence. 25 Nor did he enter heaven to offer himself again and again, the way the high priest enters the Most Holy Place every year with blood that is not his own. 26 Otherwise Christ would have had to suffer many times since the creation of the world. But he has appeared once for all at the culmination of the ages to do away with sin by the sacrifice of himself. 27 Just as people are destined to die once, and after that to face judgment, 28 so Christ was sacrificed once to take away the sins of many; and he will appear a second time, not to bear sin, but to bring salvation to those who are waiting for him.* His blood was enough—God's grace was enough!

Remember when Jesus saw Mary just outside the tomb. **John 20:17 (KJV)** *17 Jesus saith unto her, Touch me not; for I am not yet ascended to my Father: but go to my brethren, and say unto them, I ascend unto my Father, and your Father; and to my God, and your God.* He was acting as our High Priest, carrying His own blood, the perfect sacrifice, into the heavenly Holy of Holies. He poured out that blood on the altar in heaven and God the Father accepted it on our behalf. The debt is totally paid, and we have received righteousness and freedom from sin and shame.

Romans 12:1 (KJV) *1 I beseech you therefore, brethren, by the mercies of God, that ye present your bodies a living sacrifice, holy, acceptable unto God, which is your reasonable service.* Your offering is to live for Him who died for you. You owe Jesus everything. All He demands is your heart, which will produce in you a life of obedience. Lay your will on the altar and make His will your own. Walk in the freedom of that life which grace gave you.

Genesis 31:49 (KJV) *49 ... The LORD watch between me and thee, when we are absent one from another.*

Mizpah

Have you ever worn one of those broken medallions that have engraved upon them; "The Lord watch between you and me what time we are apart the one from the other." Sometimes, close friends or husbands and wives wear necklaces with that written upon them. Those words were from a covenant made in the Bible. The city where the covenant took place was called Mizpah, the watchtower.

The text comes from a covenant made between Jacob and his father-in-law, Laban. There is a lot of backstory between them. The name Jacob means deceiver and usurper, one who will take what is not his own. Jacob lived down to that name and it cost him. First of all, Jacob came to his uncle Laban because he had deceived his own father into giving him his twin brother's blessing and there was some serious hatred at home.

Once he had escaped the rage of his brother, Esau, and traveled a great distance to Laban, Jacob fell in love with Rachel. The hand of the Lord was still on Jacob, blessing what he did. So seeing that, Laban agreed to give him Rachel as a wife. Jacob, who has been a deceiver, serves faithfully for seven full years to get the woman of his dreams only to find out come morning that it is Rachel's sister

Leah he has spent the night with. I get it that Jacob is angry, but can we just give Leah a couple of minutes of our time and attention.

Leah has lived in the shadow of her younger sister for as long as she can remember. Rachel is beautiful and Leah is very ordinary. No local man has 'come calling.' She is the older sister, so when a handsome young man shows up, her heart probably leapt at the thought of him. Then he falls in love with her rival. For seven years, she watches Jacob slave for her father so he can have her sister. Then Laban has this enormous wedding and in the middle of the night he says, 'Leah, you go on in to Jacob and keep quiet and he will fall in love with you.' So she takes a chance and pours out her love to him all night long. You can just imagine the rejection that woman felt, knowing he thought he was with her sister and their one night, when she felt loved and wanted was all a hoax. She spends the rest of her life trying to win Jacob over, but he will never love her like he loves Rachel. When he sees her he does not say 'Oh my, I finally recognize that I love you Leah.' No, he screams in rage that she is not Rachel. The deceiver had himself been deceived, and poor Leah was just a pawn in the matter. Laban says we always marry off the oldest daughter first you have to give her a full week and then we can get you Rachel. I don't imagine it was much of a honeymoon for her, and Leah is replaced the moment he can marry Rachel. So he agrees to work an additional seven years to get the woman he really wanted. Then he works another seven for flocks of his own.

Life became so strained in Laban's household that Jacob decided to leave. He did not bid Laban farewell or explain why he was leaving. Jacob, his two wives, two concubines and all their children packed up and left during the night to go back to face his brother, Esau. There have been at least twenty-one years for Esau's anger to cool. Jacob dishonored his father-in-law by the way he departed. He acted the same way as when he fled Esau; Jacob, the deceiver, sneaks away in the night.

Genesis 31:22-26 (KJV) *22 And it was told Laban on the third day that Jacob was fled. 23 And he took his brethren with him, and pursued after him seven days' journey; and they overtook him in the* *mount Gilead.* When Laban and a small army pursued Jacob and his family and were almost upon them, the Lord spoke to him to do Jacob and his family no harm. *24 And God came to Laban the Syrian in a dream by night, and said unto him, Take heed that thou speak not to Jacob either good or bad. 25 Then Laban overtook Jacob. Now Jacob had pitched his tent in the mount: and Laban with his brethren pitched in the mount of Gilead. 26 And Laban said to Jacob, What hast thou done, that thou hast stolen away unawares to me, and carried away my daughters, as captives taken with the sword?* This is one very dysfunctional family. I am thinking the air is thick with anger, resentment, and jealousy. The whole time they were together was strained.

It was at this point that the covenant was established. **Genesis 31:44-55 (KJV)** *44 Now therefore come thou, let us make a covenant, I and thou; and let it be for a witness between me and thee. 45 And Jacob took a stone, and set it up for a pillar. 46 And Jacob said unto his brethren, Gather stones; and they took stones, and made an heap: and they did eat there upon the heap ... 48 And Laban said, This heap is a witness between me and thee this day. Therefore was the name of it called Galeed; 49 And Mizpah; for he said, The LORD watch between me and thee, when we are absent one from another. 50 If thou shalt afflict my daughters, or if thou shalt take other wives beside my daughters, no man is with us; see, God is witness betwixt me and thee. 51 And Laban said to Jacob, Behold this heap, and behold this pillar, which I have cast betwixt me and thee; 52 This heap be witness, and this pillar be witness, that I will not pass over this heap to thee, and that thou shalt not pass over this heap and this pillar unto me, for harm. 53 The God of Abraham, and the God of Nahor, the God of their father, judge betwixt us. And Jacob sware by the fear of his father Isaac. 54 Then Jacob offered sacrifice upon the mount, and called his brethren to eat bread: and they did eat bread, and tarried all night in the mount. 55 And early in the morning Laban rose up, and kissed his sons and his daughters, and blessed them: and Laban departed, and returned unto his place.* The main idea of Mizpah is that God is the One who watches over the covenant to make sure all are protected and kept safe.

There was a stone set up to remind the men who passed by that God was the true keeper of the covenant and that He was present to minister protection and judgement as the actions of the men involved required. Any covenant had those two parts, the blessing and the curse. The idea behind that monument was that this was a perpetual agreement; it was solid, carved in stone, so as to guarantee that those men would never forget or dishonor their commitment to one another.

Marriage should be that kind of a commitment, but for many it is not. Many, like Leah, are tormented that they are not really loved or cherished. More than any other relationship, marriage was a picture of the love God had for us. **Ephesians 5:21-32 (KJV)** *21 Submitting yourselves one to another in the fear of God. 22 Wives, submit yourselves unto your own husbands, as unto the Lord. 23 For the husband is the head of the wife, even as Christ is the head of the church: and he is the saviour of the body. 24 Therefore as the church is subject unto Christ, so let the wives be to their own husbands in every thing. 25 Husbands, love your wives, even as Christ also loved the church, and gave himself for it; 26 That he might sanctify and cleanse it with the washing of water by the word, 27 That he might present it to himself a glorious church, not having spot, or wrinkle, or any such thing; but that it should be holy and without blemish. 28 So ought men to love their wives as their own bodies. He that loveth his wife loveth himself. 29 For no man ever yet hated his own flesh; but nourisheth and cherisheth it, even as the Lord the church: 30 For we are members of his body, of his flesh, and of his bones. 31 For this cause shall a man leave his father and mother, and shall be joined unto his wife, and they two shall be one flesh. 32 This is a great mystery: but I speak concerning Christ and the church.*

We need to remember that God has a love for us that never wavers, and which will last into eternity. He did not carve it in stone this time like He did the Ten Commandments, but He wrote it on our hearts [Romans 2:29] and engraved it in the hands of our Savior. Jesus did not just work seven or fourteen years to have us, but He left the glory of heaven and came to be abused and crucified to make us a part of the bride of Christ. He loves us perfectly and He will never trick or deceive us. He will never prefer another over us or turn away from us. Jesus has established a covenant of love for us that will culminate in heaven. His undying love is our heritage. We have become His by virtue of His perfect sacrifice. The Lord of Glory, the King of Kings has chosen us as His bride. **Revelation 19:5-9 (KJV)** *5 And a voice came out of the throne, saying, Praise our God, all ye his servants, and ye that fear him, both small and great. 6 And I heard as it were the voice of a great multitude, and as the voice of many waters, and as the voice of mighty thunderings, saying, Alleluia: for the Lord God omnipotent reigneth. 7 Let us be glad and rejoice, and give honour to him: for the marriage of the Lamb is come, and his wife hath made herself ready. 8 And to her was granted that she should be arrayed in fine linen, clean and white: for the fine linen is the righteousness of saints. 9 And he saith unto me, Write, Blessed are they which are called unto the marriage supper of the Lamb. And he saith unto me, These are the true sayings of God.* We are invited to the marriage supper, not as witnesses, but as the bride. The greatest celebration in heaven will be when we sit at the table with Jesus and He is able to pour the fullness of His love upon us.

2 Corinthians 10:5 (KJV)
5Casting down imaginations, and every high thing that exalteth itself against the knowledge of God, and bringing into captivity every thought to the obedience of Christ;

Tower of Babel

There was a very real place that became known at the Tower of Babel. This is the story. **Genesis 11:1-9 (KJV)** *1 And the whole earth was of one language, and of one speech. 2 And it came to pass, as they journeyed from the east, that they found a plain in the land of Shinar; and they dwelt there. 3 And they said one to another, Go to, let us make brick, and burn them throughly. And they had brick for stone, and slime had they for morter. 4 And they said, Go to, let us build us a city and a tower, whose top may reach unto heaven; and let us make us a name, lest we be scattered abroad upon the face of the whole earth. 5 And the LORD came down to see the city and the tower, which the children of men builded. 6 And the LORD said, Behold, the people is one, and they have all one language; and this they begin to do: and now nothing will be restrained from them, which they have imagined to do. 7 Go to, let us go down, and there confound their language, that they may not understand one another's speech. 8 So the LORD scattered them abroad from thence upon the face of all the earth: and they left off to build the city. 9 Therefore is the name of it called Babel; because the LORD did there confound the language of all the earth: and from thence did the LORD scatter them abroad upon the face of all the earth.* Since the people lost their focus and sense of purpose, and became incapable of communicating with one another, all confusion can be traced back to this event.

It was at the Tower of Babel that frustration and confusion and failure seemed to take over the inner thoughts of men. I am not as interested in that stone tower, as I am with the talk in your head. It is that inner confusion that puts most of us in a state of hopelessness. We self-talk all the time. There is a constant voice in the mind and spirit of man. Not the kind that the psychiatrist asks about, just a normal self-doubting discouraged, nagging and confused inner us. It is the one you hear that sounds like that critical teacher or even your mother. It is the one that says you cannot succeed and the one that questions your intents and actions. It is also the one that speaks just as you are going to sleep, "You forgot to take that book to Betty last week—get up and lay it out so you will remember in the morning." Or "You have that appointment this week. What are you going to wear?" "You can't wear the black dress you wore that last time you saw them and that blue one is dirty. You should have done the laundry instead of typing all day." It is frequently the condemning voice that says you didn't really pray about that need your friend mentioned. It is the voice that reminds you of every harsh word you have spoken and those hard words that were spoken to you. It is the one that says your pants are too tight, and your shirt is all wrong and everyone thinks you are fat and undisciplined. In my case it often says things like, "Why did you eat that, you know you aren't really hungry." "No one wants to read your silly ramblings; you don't have anything to say that matters to people." "You are going to end up with a pile of books in the bedroom." "People are going to find out you don't know enough and aren't good enough and then no one will even care about you." Most of the time, we act as if we do not hear the voice babbling away in our head. Our fears, insecurities and sometimes even our facial expressions show that it is still there.

After I became a sign language interpreter, I actually caught myself fingerspelling my inner thoughts while I walked to my car after work. Don't try to tell me we don't hear those voices, one of them told me how stupid I looked spelling out my own fears and frustrations in sign language that other people could literally read.

When we get saved we can add the voice of the Holy Spirit to the mix, but He is a gentleman and will never completely block out all the other voices we hear. His words are always encouraging and based upon the written Word. He speaks calm, faith filled and hopeful words that have the potential to lift us out of bondage.

Freedom is not based upon circumstances; it is based on our perception of the circumstances. The three Hebrew children were free while walking around inside the fire. Paul was free while he was in prison, or we would not have most of the New Testament. John was free on the Isle of Patmos. You are free right now; God made you free, and regardless of the circumstances in your life, you do not have to be bound. You choose how you think about what is happening around you and your thoughts matter. They affect your behavior. If we are free within ourselves we can be locked in a jail cell and still never feel trapped. However, if we are imprisoned in our minds, we can be sitting on a beach and still not enjoy any sense freedom.

When my husband was drinking and didn't want me because I was 'too saved' for him, he made me feel hopeless and lost and rejected. He left me four times. I felt like I had the word FAILURE stamped on my forehead. All that was strong and secure in my life had crumbled and I was left in a pile of debris. I was a Christian and a minister. My marriage was supposed to be strong, and I didn't believe in divorce. I grew up believing in the forever kind of love. Buzz finally did file for divorce, but it was God who helped me to hold my head high while I learned to really trust in Him. On one of my darkest days, God showed me in the Word that He had already covered my loneliness and failure. **Isaiah 54:5 - 6 (KJV)** *5 For thy Maker is thine husband; the LORD of hosts is his name; and thy Redeemer the Holy One of Israel; The God of the whole earth shall he be called. 6 For the LORD hath called thee as a woman forsaken and grieved in spirit, and a wife of youth, when thou wast refused, saith thy God.* Something broke that day that let me breathe again. I wasn't thinking the same things. I no longer felt hopeless. God would be my covering. I would not be all alone, God would be with me. My circumstances had not changed but my attitude and my self-talk had. That constant babble of failure and rejection was silenced. That is, after all, the most important victory, the one we have in the spirit. Our inner man must be free.

When life was too overwhelming to face, God stood with me. I had peace in the midst of the storm. About the time the divorce would have been final, God changed everything. My husband got saved. He was set free and came home. God has fully restored our marriage. God healed our relationship so perfectly, it is as if that time of brokenness never even happened to me personally. It is like the memory of a movie I had watched, not a trauma I had endured. God is no respecter of persons. What He did for me, He will do for you and your circumstances. We are all broken and trapped and damaged in some way but He has it all worked out. When the doubts are shouting at you, remind yourself that God loves you and has a plan to bring you into victory. **Jeremiah 29:11 (NIV)** *11 For I know the plans I have for you, declares the LORD, plans to prosper you and not to harm you, plans to give you hope and a future.*

2 Corinthians 10:4 -5 (KJV) *4(For the weapons of our warfare are not carnal, but mighty through God to the pulling down of strong holds;) 5 <u>Casting down imaginations, and every high thing that exalteth itself against the knowledge of God, and bringing into captivity every thought to the obedience of Christ;</u>* Notice the understood subject of that sentence is "You." While it is still just a thought, before it can root and become a stronghold, you cast down that imagination. You decide not to wallow in despair. You look at what the Word of God says and agree with it. "You reject the imaginations and thoughts that would place themselves in authority above God's Word. Every thought is governed by what the Word says." (Copeland, p.46) If you put enough Scripture in your head it will get into your heart and become the standard you use to decide if things are right or wrong. "As you feed your mind on the Word of God, it becomes like a carefully programmed computer. You feed your mind the truth from God's Word and when information comes into your mind contrary to the Word, your mind deliberately casts it out." (Copeland, p.46) **Isaiah 55:6-9 (KJV)** *6 Seek ye the LORD while he may be found, call ye upon him while he is near: 7 <u>Let the wicked forsake his way, and the unrighteous man his thoughts</u>: and let him return unto the LORD, and he will have mercy upon him; and to our God, for he will abundantly pardon. 8 For my thoughts are not your thoughts, neither are your ways my ways, saith the LORD. 9 For as the heavens are higher than the earth, so are my ways higher than your ways, and my thoughts than your thoughts.* Notice it says you forsake those thoughts, you cast them down, and you reject what is negative and ungodly. "Your challenge on the inside is to arrest imaginations and thoughts that are destructive and contrary to God's purpose." (Edmond, p. 42) Instead of a stone in the hand of one who would throw it at you, you take that thought in hand, and you intentionally throw it away from you. You cast it aside, toss it out of sight and mind. That thought that opposes you needs to be cast away.

You train your mind to think as it should, you make God's thoughts your thoughts. No one else is responsible for what you do. You cast down those imaginations. You forget the past and move forward one day at a time. You are responsible for your thoughts. You are not a victim, a mistake or a failure; you are a child of God. You decide to shut down all that babble.

Romans 8:5-6 (KJV) *5 For they that are after the flesh do mind the things of the flesh; but they that are after the Spirit the things of the Spirit. 6 For to be carnally minded is death; but to be spiritually minded is life and peace.* If you think like the world, you will get bad results. "Be cautious of the thorns of life. The cares of this world, deceitfulness of riches, the lusts of other things, are dangerous weapons of the enemy. They enter into the heart and choke the Word until the Word cannot produce." (Copeland, p.99) You take the initiative to counter worldly thoughts with the Word of God.

James 4:7-10 (KJV) *7 Submit yourselves therefore to God. Resist the devil, and he will flee from you. 8 Draw nigh to God,* *and he will draw nigh to you. Cleanse your hands, ye sinners; and purify your hearts, ye double minded. 9 Be afflicted, and mourn, and weep: let your laughter be turned to mourning, and your joy to heaviness. 10 Humble yourselves in the sight of the Lord, and he shall lift you up.* We choose how close we are to God. We give ourselves completely to Him, or we do not. The scripture here says first you surrender yourself to God. You submit, that is, you yield your will to His. After we have done that we can resist the devil and he will have to flee. We have to purposefully choose to do things God's way. We can stay filled with His fire and His presence or we can walk completely away or even follow from afar. We have a will and a choice.

Psalm 37:3-7 (KJV) *3 Trust in the LORD, and do good; so shalt thou dwell in the land, and verily thou shalt be fed. 4 Delight thyself also in the LORD; and he shall give thee the desires of thine heart. 5 Commit thy way unto the LORD; trust also in him; and he shall bring it to pass. 6 And he shall bring forth thy righteousness as the light, and thy judgment as the noonday. 7 Rest in the LORD, and wait patiently for him: fret not thyself because of him who prospereth in his way, because of the man who bringeth wicked devices to pass.* Don't worry about who is right and wrong. Don't waste time comparing yourself, your life or your problems to others. You make God the center of your life. You delight in Him. And He who has become the desire of your heart will fulfill it. Silence all the garbage, and just rest in the One who loves you so very much.

Perception is everything. Did you know that when a circus has a baby elephant they chain it up by the leg with a pretty strong chain to a deeply set post so it can't escape? It struggles so hard to be free that it sometimes hurts its leg. It is only chained like that for a short time, but later in life all they have to do is wrap a small chain around its foot to keep it from running away. The chain is not even attached to a post, and while the elephant has grown big enough to escape even the large chain, it remembers struggling against the chain and it is bound in its mind and won't try to escape. The devil can't hold you. He doesn't have the power to overtake you, but if you believe you are stuck where you are—then you are. You have to see yourself free. You have to know who you are and that you are capable of walking out of that prison.

Isaiah 26:3 (KJV) *3 Thou wilt keep him in perfect peace, whose mind is stayed on thee: because he trusteth in thee.* Get your heart and your mind on God and it won't really matter what is going on around you. You are loved and accepted and the price for all your sin and failure is paid. Why do you walk around as if you are condemned when He has already set you free? Why do you let your past control you? Once you were saved, everything was covered by the blood. There is no record in heaven of your sins and failures. God has preordained that you walk in the freedom Jesus purchased for you. If you will just let Him have control, He will bring you both freedom and peace. **John 14:27 (KJV)** *27 Peace I leave with you, my peace I give unto you: not as the world giveth, give I unto you. Let not your heart be troubled, neither let it be afraid.*

When the voice of criticism and condemnation comes, when the fear and insecurity try to scream that you are nothing and you are no one, remember that God valued you so highly that He willingly sent Jesus to the cross in your place. The Lord of Glory thought you were worth dying for. He poured out blood for you and it is you that He has set His heart upon. You have great value. You are precious and priceless and you are free to walk in that knowledge. You are no longer a slave to fear and hopelessness. You are loved—you are free—walk in that knowledge.

Philippians 3:13-14 (KJV) *13 Brethren, I count not myself to have apprehended: but this one thing I do, forgetting those things which are behind, and reaching forth unto those things which are before, 14 I press toward the mark for the prize of the high calling of God in Christ Jesus.*

Stones in the Jordan

If anyone had a right to rejoice over their victories, it would have been Moses and the children of Israel. They could have sat down next to the Red Sea, to relish their victory, but they would never have found the Promised Land. They did not sit upon their laurels, they kept walking. Neither did they sit at the foot of Mt. Zion remembering the fire on the mountain. That was glorious but it was not their destination. They kept going and when the time came to enter the Promised Land, Joshua led them forward. They went right through the Jordan River just like they did the Red Sea. They did establish a memorial, but they did not stop there.

Deuteronomy 27:1-8 (KJV) *1 And Moses with the elders of Israel commanded the people, saying, Keep all the commandments which I command you this day. 2 And it shall be on the day when ye shall pass over Jordan unto the land which the LORD thy God giveth thee, that thou shalt set thee up great stones, and plaister them with plaister: 3 And thou shalt write upon them all the words of this law, when thou art passed over, that thou mayest go in unto the land which the LORD thy God giveth thee, a land that floweth with milk and honey; as the LORD God of thy fathers hath promised thee. 4 Therefore it shall be when ye be gone over Jordan, that ye shall set up these stones, which I command you this day, in mount Ebal, and* *thou shalt plaister them with plaister. 5 And there shalt thou build an altar unto the LORD thy God, an altar of stones: thou shalt not lift up any iron tool upon them. 6 Thou shalt build the altar of the LORD thy God of whole stones: and thou shalt offer burnt offerings thereon unto the LORD thy God: 7 And thou shalt offer peace offerings, and shalt eat there, and rejoice before the LORD thy God. 8 And thou shalt write upon the stones all the words of this law very plainly.*

The children of Israel didn't get it right the first time they got to the Jordan. They turned back and roamed around in the desert for forty years until all of the fearful and unbelieving men died off. But they did come back to that place and set up their memorial.

Joshua 3:11-17 (KJV) *11 Behold, the ark of the covenant of the Lord of all the earth passeth over before you into Jordan. 12 Now therefore take you twelve men out of the tribes of Israel, out of every tribe a man. 13 And it shall come to pass, as soon as the soles of the feet of the priests that bear the ark of the LORD, the Lord of all the earth, shall rest in the waters of Jordan, that the waters of Jordan shall be cut off from the waters that come down from above; and they shall stand upon an heap. 14 And it came to pass, when the people removed from their tents, to pass over Jordan, and the priests bearing the ark of the covenant before the people; 15 And as they that bare the ark were come unto Jordan, and the feet of the priests that bare the ark were dipped in the brim of the water, (for Jordan overfloweth all his banks all the time of harvest,) 16 That the waters which came down from above stood and rose up upon an heap very far from the city Adam, that is beside Zaretan: and those that came down toward the sea of the plain, even the salt sea, failed, and were cut off: and the people passed over right against Jericho. 17 And the priests that bare the ark of the covenant of the LORD stood firm on dry ground in the midst of Jordan, and all the Israelites passed over on dry ground, until all the people were passed clean over Jordan.* Only God makes a way through the river like that. That miracle did not go unnoticed. It was an entrance that the inhabitants of the land saw. Great fear was upon their enemies because God was so obviously with the Israelites. So they set up a memorial to call attention to the mighty work of God.

Joshua 4:3-9 (KJV) *3 And command ye them, saying, Take you hence out of the midst of Jordan, out of the place where the priests' feet stood firm, twelve stones, and ye shall carry them over with you, and leave them in the lodging place, where ye shall lodge this night. 4 Then Joshua called the twelve men, whom he had prepared of the children of Israel, out of every tribe a man: 5 And Joshua said unto them, Pass over before the ark of the LORD your God into the midst of Jordan, and take ye up every man of you a stone upon his shoulder, according unto the number of the tribes of the children of Israel: 6 That this may be a sign among you, that when your children ask their fathers in time to come, saying, What mean ye by these stones? 7 Then ye shall answer them, That the waters of Jordan were cut off before the ark of the covenant of the LORD; when it passed over Jordan, the waters of Jordan were cut off: and these stones shall be for a memorial unto the children of Israel for ever. 8 And the children of Israel did so as Joshua commanded, and took up twelve stones out of the midst of Jordan, as the LORD spake unto Joshua, according to the number of the tribes of the children of Israel, and carried them over with them unto the place where they lodged, and laid them down there. 9 And Joshua set up twelve stones in the midst of Jordan, in the place where the feet of the priests which bare the ark of the covenant stood: and they are there unto this day.*

It is right to acknowledge success and remember the good, but that memory should never become a place where we park and set up a shrine to our achievement and rejoice in our good deeds and never leave. We can't let a memorial freeze us into inaction, while we admire our trophies.

Daniel didn't spend the rest of his days thinking about the night he slept with the lions. The three Hebrew children did not camp out at the furnace where they escaped the flames of the enemy and walked with the Lord. Even Peter, James and John, who stood on the Mountain of Transfiguration and saw Jesus shine with the glory of God, couldn't stay there. **Matthew 17:1-5 (KJV)** *1 And after six days Jesus taketh Peter, James, and John his brother, and bringeth them up into an high mountain apart, 2 And was transfigured before* *them: and his face did shine as the sun, and his raiment was white as the light. 3 And, behold, there appeared unto them Moses and Elias talking with him. 4 Then answered Peter, and said unto Jesus, Lord, it is good for us to be here: if thou wilt, let us make here three tabernacles; one for thee, and one for Moses, and one for Elias.* Peter wanted to just set up camp there. *5 While he yet spake, behold, a bright cloud overshadowed them: and behold a voice out of the cloud, which said, This is my beloved Son, in whom I am well pleased; hear ye him.* God said, 'Get it together Peter, and listen to Jesus.'

Just like Peter, we sometimes want to set up camp at the place of our last encounter with God. We are willing to get stagnate by staying there. We like that good memory, and so we tend to memorialize it; we would build a monument and stay there. Those are good things but they are in the past. Do what David did, when you need to, look back long enough to see the victory and encourage yourself in the Lord and then move on. **1 Samuel 30:3-6 (KJV)** *3 So David and his men came to the city, and, behold, it was burned with fire; and their wives, and their sons, and their daughters, were taken captives. 4 Then David and the people that were with him lifted up their voice and wept, until they had no more power to weep. 5 And David's two wives were taken captives, Ahinoam the Jezreelitess, and Abigail the wife of Nabal the Carmelite. 6 And David was greatly distressed; for the people spake of stoning him, because the soul of all the people was grieved, every man for his sons and for his daughters: but David encouraged himself in the LORD his God.* David found comfort in what God had done for him before. It gave him the strength to go to war again and recover what was lost.

David made it a habit to look back, and see the past victory until he was motivated to move into his next fight. He did it when facing Goliath. **1 Samuel 17:32-37 (KJV)** *32 And David said to Saul, Let no man's heart fail because of him; thy servant will go and fight with this Philistine. 33 And Saul said to David, Thou art not able to go against this Philistine to fight with him: for thou art but a youth, and he a man of war from his youth. 34 And David said unto*

Saul, Thy servant kept his father's sheep, and there came a lion, and a bear, and took a lamb out of the flock: 35 And I went out after him, and smote him, and delivered it out of his mouth: and when he arose against me, I caught him by his beard, and smote him, and slew him. 36 Thy servant slew both the lion and the bear: and this uncircumcised Philistine shall be as one of them, seeing he hath defied the armies of the living God. 37 David said moreover, The LORD that delivered me out of the paw of the lion, and out of the paw of the bear, he will deliver me out of the hand of this Philistine. And Saul said unto David, Go, and the LORD be with thee. David used his past to form a strong image of success in his present, and it helped him to reach a positive future.

He did the same thing when he was fleeing from King Saul. **1 Samuel 21:9 (KJV)** *9 And the priest said, The sword of Goliath the Philistine, whom thou slewest in the valley of Elah, behold, it is here wrapped in a cloth behind the ephod: if thou wilt take that, take it: for there is no other save that here. And David said, There is none like that; give it me.* He said, 'That is the sword of my old enemy Goliath. God and I defeated him together. It is proof that God is with me.' Again, he encouraged himself in the Lord. He did not sit down and camp out at the place of victory, but he used it to move himself forward.

I am proud that I did some things well in life. I have seen miracles; I have preached in conferences and written two other books. I was valedictorian in Bible College. I sang on local TV. I interpreted for both President George W. Bush and Senator Obama. Signing made a way for me to stand on stage with Evangelist Bennie Hinn, and music legends Diamond Rio and The Oak Ridge Boys. I have played an integral part in earning lots of bachelor degrees for various students. I have made some beautiful wedding gowns, and several nice quilts. I have a flare for decorating and have helped others with their homes. I helped run a soup kitchen, and a food pantry to minister to the needy. I have some places where I can look back and be thankful that God blessed me as He did. As long as I live, I hope to be useful and I want to add to my successes and learn from my failures and just keep pressing on.

You do not always win, and you do not always lose. Regardless of your past failures and successes, you are not finished running your course. **Philippians 3:13-14 (KJV)** *13 Brethren, I count not myself to have apprehended: but this one thing I do, forgetting those things which are behind, and reaching forth unto those things which are before, 14 I press toward the mark for the prize of the high calling of God in Christ Jesus.* Use your past victories but do not dwell on them.

Acknowledge your moments of triumph and maybe even set up a stone marker so you can go back occasionally to encourage yourself in the Lord. Do not stay for an extended visit; you have new territory to travel. He is with you to bring you into a place of victory. The Lord is your helper, and you are His own beloved bride. Do not be afraid—do not be consumed with either victory or defeat. Know to whom you belong and press on.

They Could Have Stoned Her

Tamar was an Old Testament Canaanite woman who was wronged and who risked being stoned to death in order to bear an heir for her husband. Tamar was willing to go to drastic measures to receive what was legally hers. She would not be denied.

Judah was a Hebrew, but he married outside of his clan which meant outside of the covenant between God and Abraham. He also sought a bride for his eldest son outside of his faith. **Genesis 38:6-11 (KJV)** *6 And Judah took a wife for Er his firstborn, whose name was Tamar. 7 And Er, Judah's firstborn, was wicked in the sight of the LORD; and the LORD slew him.* The name Tamar meant Palm tree, or one who is fruitful, and yet she did not bear any children during the time she and Er were wed. The Bible says Er was wicked, so they probably did not have a good life together. It also indicates that he died as a result of divine judgment. For some reason, God thought him unworthy to remain on this earth; he must have been quite evil. *8 And Judah said unto Onan, Go in unto thy brother's wife, and marry her, and raise up seed to thy brother. 9 And Onan knew that the seed should not be his; and it came to pass, when* *he went in unto his brother's wife, that he spilled it on the ground, lest that he should give seed to his brother.* By doing what he did, Onan disobeyed custom and the direct command of his father. In addition, he also dishonored his father, his brother, and Tamar. He did not refuse to have relations with her but he was determined to deny her a child. *10 And the thing which he did displeased the LORD: wherefore he slew him also.* Judah now has two sons cut down early in life by the hand of God. I am sure Judah's Canaanite wife blamed Tamar for the death of her two eldest sons. Tamar had been innocent and is now a widow at the mercy of a family that is broken and grieving. Tamar was probably only about fourteen when she was taken as a wife for Er, and even if a few years have come and gone she is still a young girl. *11 Then said Judah to Tamar his daughter-in-law, Remain a widow at thy father's house, till Shelah my son be grown: for he said, Lest peradventure he die also, as his brethren did. And Tamar went and dwelt in her father's house.* Being sent back to her father's home is another insult. They would not even keep her under their roof until their youngest son was ready for marriage. That probably made her suspicious that she would not be called back at all, and there is no doubt she felt totally rejected.

By both Hebrew and Canaanite law, the brother of her husband was responsible to bring honor to the dead by providing an heir. It was also acceptable to the Canaanites for her father-in-law or another close relative to take her in order to bring forth a son to keep the family name alive. It was not a strange thing to have the family blended in order to produce a descendent for the man who died. In this case Tamar was just sent away to wait for the youngest son to mature with the promise that one day he would marry her and give an heir to Er. That never happened, and eventually she took matters into her own hands.

Genesis 38:12-17 (KJV) *12 And in process of time the daughter of Shuah Judah's wife died; and Judah was comforted, and went up unto his sheepshearers to Timnath, he and his friend Hirah the Adullamite. 13 And it was told Tamar, saying, Behold thy father-in-law goeth up to Timnath to shear his sheep.* Tamar grew weary of waiting for Judah to do what was right by her. Shelah was fully grown and had not married her, so she formulated a plan to conceive a child. *14 And she put her widow's garments off from her, and covered her with a vail, and wrapped herself, and sat in an open place, which is by the way to Timnath; for she saw that Shelah was grown, and she was not given unto him to wife.* Just because she dressed like a prostitute was no guarantee that her father-in-law would choose to spend intimate time with her. She was making it possible for Judah to sleep with her. She hoped that she would conceive. The trap was set, and the rest depended upon Judah. She put her future in God's hands. It was her right and her obligation to produce a son for her late husband. She was more concerned about the legality of what she did, than the moral issue at hand. *15 When Judah saw her, he thought her to be an harlot; because she had covered her face. 16 And he turned unto her by the way, and said, Go to, I pray thee, let me come in unto thee; (for he knew not that she was his daughter-in-law.) And she said, What wilt thou give me, that thou mayest come in unto me? 17 And he said, I will send thee a kid from the flock. And she said, Wilt thou give me a pledge, till thou send it? 18 And he said, What pledge shall I give thee? And she said, Thy signet, and thy bracelets, and thy staff that is in thine hand.* Each item she asked for was proof of identification. A walking stick was his identification as head of a clan; his signet was the carved seal he used for legal documents and sealing letters. If her plan worked and she became pregnant she would be stoned to death unless she could make Judah take responsibility for the child. These items would be unmistakably his. *And he gave it her, and came in unto her, and she conceived by him.* She knew Judah would never marry her to his youngest son. She would not bear Er a child through Shelah and Judah had not provided any other near relative for that purpose and so she tricked him. Tamar would not be denied the child that would become her husband's heir and secure her future. She was taking by deceit what was rightfully hers, while Judah was only taking pleasure in sin. He thought he was with a stranger, paying for sexual favor. He was unaware that the whole time it was part of a plan to bring him an heir.

Genesis 38:24-26 (KJV) *24 And it came to pass about three months after, that it was told Judah, saying, Tamar thy daughter-in-law hath played the harlot; and also, behold, she is with child by whoredom. And Judah said, Bring her forth, and let her be burnt.* Normally, the punishment for an unfaithful wife was stoning. He must have thought that stoning was too swift, too good for his daughter-in-law who had so shamed his family. He wanted her to die slowly and in great agony for carrying the child of what he thought was whoredom. *25 When she was brought forth, she sent to her father-in-law, saying, By the man, whose these are, am I with child: and she said, Discern, I pray thee, whose are these, the signet, and bracelets, and staff. 26 And Judah acknowledged them, and said, She hath been more righteous than I; because that I gave her not to Shelah my son. And he knew her again no more.* She could have died doing what she did. If she did not conceive, she would have had to live with the guilt of her night of deception, but no one else would have known. Sometimes the risk is worth it; for Tamar it was. She bore not one son, but twins. Her method was wrong, but in the end, God used it. She risked everything to bring an heir to Judah and his son Er, and for that she became one of a handful of women in the lineage of Christ.

Throughout her story we see Tamar wronged. She was given to a harsh husband who was so evil God struck him dead. She is then given to his brother, who is much kinder, but who also has his own agenda and makes her a widow a second time. She is sent home in shame to her father's house to wait for years while Shelah grew more mature so she could have the child she was promised. She would be justified in feeling both desperate and discarded. A widow without a son had no hope in her society. Her father would not care for her forever. After she resorted to desperate measures, she was judged as an adulteress and almost killed. Do you see how all those stones of offence can stack up and wall her into despair? Every time a wrong was done to her it could have closed her off, imprisoned her in her sorrow. Tamar could have given up along the way and just wallowed in self-pity and grief, but she chose not to do that. Somehow she had to find her way out of that place if she really wanted to have peace in her heart. Since she was to live in Judah's home from that day forward, she had to forgive all of the past to enjoy peace in her future.

Our pastor teaches that withholding forgiveness is dangerous. Our bitterness and resentment damages us more than the one who offended us. He says holding a grudge is like taking poison and then expected the other person to die. The condition of our heart is much more important than any supposed wrong done to us. We must forgive for our own spiritual well-being.

I understand that very well. I too, had a few harsh, hurtful experiences. When I got saved I came out of most of them, but there were still stumbling stones on my path. I noticed there were hurtful reminders that I had been wronged and that no one really understood. So, shortly after I was saved, I decided to forgive. Not just a quiet inner decision, but a quality decision that required I send word to my tormentor to tell him I forgive him. He had date raped me. That was something almost no one knew, but because Jesus forgave me and healed that place in me, I had to forgive him. He had rejected me when I was pregnant, but the Lord had shown me grace, so again I forgave him. He had told me to abort my precious daughter, but God had not only blessed me with a wonderful daughter, but had given me a new husband to help raise her. So, after looking at the Word of God and gathering all my faith and courage, I called the woman who would have become my sister-in-law and told her to pass on the word of forgiveness. I told her I was happy and healthy and that my daughter was a treasure. I told her I didn't want anyone to think I hated them. I told her I had married a good man and that I had found Christ and that I needed to forgive all the wrongs done to me so I could move on. I was truly at peace when I hung up that phone. There were no longer any stumbling stones of bitterness or resentment lying across my path; it was clean and smooth.

There is something very freeing in letting go of past hurt. I forgave because it was the right thing to do. I forgave because I read that if I would not forgive others it blocked the forgiveness

I needed. **Matthew 6:14-15 (KJV)** *14 For if ye forgive men their trespasses, your heavenly Father will also forgive you: 15 But if ye forgive not men their trespasses, neither will your Father forgive your trespasses.*

I chose to forgive, as a conscious committed act of obedience to my Lord. I made a quality decision to forgive. It did not matter if the one I forgave deserved to be forgiven, or understood why I forgave him, or even cared if I forgave him. The feelings were not important; the opinions of others were not important. However, acting as Christ had toward me mattered very much. We never forgive based on merit or feelings. We forgive because we have been forgiven and nothing else will ever matter as much as the blood poured out for us or the grace and peace that filled us. We forgive as much for our own good as for the one who injured us. There is great victory in letting go of past hurt. And having forgiven, we see the prison walls of self-pity and sorrow all fall down.

Roll the Stone Away

The worst prisons are those in the mind and spirit where we wall ourselves in with fear and shame and self-doubt and fail to see that the blood already set us free. We imprison ourselves, by condemning ourselves to live in that dark, dead place. That sounds like a tomb, but we can come out of that place. Jesus already took our place and He has rolled away the stone that kept us trapped in our past.

Galatians 2:20 (KJV) *20 I am crucified with Christ: nevertheless I live; yet not I, but Christ liveth in me: and the life which I now live in the flesh I live by the faith of the Son of God, who loved me, and gave himself for me.* I think of it like this. I was trapped in the past, under the weight of sin and judgment—condemned because of sin. The wages of sin was death, and in the realm of the eternal that meant death on the cross. Sin had me lying across the wooden beam, the nail poised to go into my flesh, when Jesus got between me and the nails. He assumed my guilt; Jesus bore my sin so perfectly that I was there with Him. By faith, I died on that cross. My sins were there, He took them into his own body on the tree, and when He died, I died to those sins. They were paid for. I am no longer carrying the weight of them. Men lay His body in a stone tomb. They sealed the door with a huge round stone that fell into a deep notch that held it firmly in place. Everything I had ever done, every sin, all my failure, and all the wrongs done to me were buried in that grave. All of my grief, and sorrow and every form of loss were placed there. He rose victorious over death, and when He did, I came out of my own tomb. Jesus did not roll away the stone so He could leave the tomb. He rolled away the stone so I could see there was nothing left behind of the sin and bondage buried in Christ. He rolled away the stone so I could go free.

2 Corinthians 5:17-18 (KJV) *17 Therefore if any man be in Christ, he is a new creature: old things are passed away; behold, all things are become new. 18 And all things are of God, who hath reconciled us to himself by Jesus Christ, and hath given to us the ministry of reconciliation;* Sin and guilt built walls to keep us entombed, but faith in what Jesus did will turn them to rubble. God never intended for us to walk around with our sins and failures firmly in place. No, He set us free—not by hiding our sins, but by completely removing them from us and making us into something entirely new. When you were born again you were not just cleaned up, you became a totally different person. The old man is dead and buried. You have a brand new life, a clean slate; you walk out of that tomb free.

When I was about five years old, I remember waking up in the middle of the night, and trying to get out of bed to go to the bathroom. I remember it being really dark. I started to get out of bed but I felt a wall to my right, which should have been the open side of the bed. It seemed odd that it was blocked. So I reached out toward the head of the bed, and there was another wall. When I turned around and felt to my left, I found solid wall again and I reached for the foot of the bed and there was another wall. It seemed like there was a solid wall on every side of me. I frantically reached out again, and I still remember the rough sand paint that scraped at my fingers as I tried to escape. I started to cry because I felt like I was trapped. I was just turned around and confused in the dark, but my Dad came in and turned on the light so I could see that I was free the whole time. Believing you are walled in makes for a strong prison. Jesus, the light of the world has come to shine into your dark places and let you know you are already free. When we know we are free, we can walk around those walls and watch them fall like the walls of Jericho did. By faith, we take the freedom that is already ours. God is on our side and He said we are free.

Romans 8:1-2 (KJV) *1 There is therefore now no condemnation to them which are in Christ Jesus, who walk not after the flesh, but after the Spirit. 2 For the law of the Spirit of life in Christ Jesus hath made me free from the law of sin and death.* There is now, no condemnation. There may have been sin, sorrow, guilt, pain and maybe even condemnation in the past, but we live in the now! We can never change what happened in our past but we can put it under the blood of Jesus. We can take the list of our sins and hurts, and make sure that the blood washes over each of them. When the enemy comes to remind us of our past and tries to crush us under with the weight of what we have done, and even what others have done to us, we can know that it has vanished. All of our sin is gone. Every hurtful memory and all the sorrow that was attached to it has been paid for and the power of it was destroyed over 2000 years ago.

I know a woman whose son is in prison for murder. She spent years trapped in her own emotional prison because her son chose a life of drugs and crime that eventually led to murder. She had not sinned. She committed no crime, but she suffered as if it were her guilt. She usurped, adopted, and assumed his guilt but it did not lighten his sentence or his sin debt. She bore what was not hers to bear; she could not get past it. She replayed the facts over and over. She feared others would judge and condemn her for what he did. Her son's sin was constantly on her mind. It was never her debt to pay and God never meant for her to carry the weight of it. But she chained herself to that one moment in time as if it defined her. That dark place in her past held her captive for a very long time. It is only through the grace of God that she has knocked down those self-imposed prison walls. She finally knows it was not her fault, and that no one has the right to judge her for what happened. She knows now that Jesus paid not only for the sin her son committed but also for the attached shame that came with it.

Isaiah 53:1 (KJV) *1Who hath believed our report? and to whom is the arm of the LORD revealed?* The only one who has really seen the power of God is the one who believes it. Believe that you are free, and you become free. Believe that you are forgiven because it is true; you have been totally forgiven. We have to live in the now, in the day of salvation. We have to remember that what is dead and buried in the sea of forgetfulness has no power over us. Regret is your past trying to steal today! We only start living when we accept the offer of salvation; we are no longer bound to the sins from our past. "Satan will try to throw obstacles and problem at you to see if he can get you trapped in another valley of sin, he'll try to defeat you by putting you in the valley of past mistakes. He'll try to bog you down in guilt and condemnation." (Hagin Jr. p. 4) You can never walk forward as you should when you are constantly looking back. You cannot afford to focus on what is behind you, what you could have or should have done. Keep your eyes on God. Trust that He, who forgave you, will continually keep you.

Romans 12:2 (KJV) *2 And be not conformed to this world: but be ye transformed by the renewing of your mind, that ye may prove what is that good, and acceptable, and perfect, will of God.* "If you are still depressed, you are conformed to the world…If you can't look people in the eye and talk to them, love them, and share with them openly, you are still conformed to the world." (Treat, p. 21) Do not stay in the state you were in. There was a great exchange that caused a spiritual transformation. The sinner became the righteous by virtue of the blood of Jesus and faith in that blood. You take hold of that truth. Be transformed. "The Greek word is metamorpho. It is a complete, total change. It means ceasing to be one thing and becoming another." (Treat, p. 22) When you were born again you stopped being a sinner and became a new person with God inside; you are never the same again. You changed like a caterpillar that became a butterfly; you are a new creature. The scripture above says you are changed by renewing your mind. You think differently than before. You look at the Word of God, and knowing it is true, you change your thinking to line up with what God has said.

2 Corinthians 5:17 (KJV) *17 Therefore if any man be in Christ, he is a new creature: old things are passed away; behold, all things are become new.* "A Christian who has been 'transformed by the renewing of his mind' bases his life on the Word of God. His feelings, experiences, or other circumstances do not change what he believes or how he acts. The Word is his foundation and guide." (Treat, p. 85) There must be a standard, a foundation that can never be shaken. For us, that standard and foundation is the Bible. We believe God's Word and hold to it knowing it will never change. It is strong enough to uphold us. I believe it was Kenneth Hagin who said, "I am not moved by what I see. I am not moved by how I feel. I am only moved by what I believe." What we believe has the power to set us free.

That does not mean you are perfect. It does not even mean you will never sin again. It does mean that when you sin, you go back to the same place where you got free. Go back to the cross and apply that same holy blood to your sin. You allow it to be covered there.

You do not have to let the circumstances in your life beat you down. Any time you are full of sorrow or regret, come back to Jesus. He has promised to give you rest. **Psalm 23:3 (KJV)** *3 He restoreth my soul: he leadeth me in the paths of righteousness for his name's sake.* The past is over, but there will be conflicts again. **John 16:33 (KJV)** *33 These things I have spoken unto you, that in me ye might have peace. In the world ye shall have tribulation: but be of good cheer; I have overcome the world.* He overcame the world, but trouble will come. Both the conflict and the victory were part of the promise. **2 Corinthians 4:8-9 (KJV)** *8 We are troubled on every side, yet not distressed; we are perplexed, but not in despair; 9 Persecuted, but not forsaken; cast down, but not destroyed;* Cling to the One who loves you best, the One who loved you first and the One who bore your sin and distress. He will get you through the things that oppose you today.

We have already said that Jesus came out of the grave unaided. He rolled away the stone. Let's look at another grave and another stone rolled away. Jesus had a dear friend named Lazarus. **John 11:3-4 (KJV)** *3 Therefore his sisters sent unto him, saying, Lord, behold, he whom thou lovest is sick. 4 When Jesus heard that, he said, This sickness is not unto death, but for the glory of God, that the Son of God might be glorified thereby.* Jesus did not rush to his side, or speak healing words to him from where He was. He waited for God's timing. Eventually, Lazarus died from his illness. **John 11:11 (KJV)** *11 ... Our friend Lazarus sleepeth; but I go, that I may awake him out of sleep.* **John 11:14-15 (KJV)** *14 Then said Jesus unto them plainly, Lazarus is dead. 15 And I am glad for your sakes that I was not there, to the intent ye may believe; nevertheless let us go unto him.*

When Jesus arrived the mourners were still present. **John 11:20-21 (KJV)** *20 Then Martha, as soon as she heard that Jesus was coming, went and met him: but Mary sat still in the house. 21 Then said Martha unto Jesus, Lord, if thou hadst been here, my brother had not died.* That almost seems like an accusation. But look at what Jesus said to her. **John 11:23-27 (KJV)** *23 Jesus saith unto her, Thy brother shall rise again. 24 Martha saith unto him, I know that he shall rise again in the resurrection at the last day. 25 Jesus said unto her, I am the resurrection, and the life: he that believeth in me, though he were dead, yet shall he live: 26 And whosoever liveth and believeth in me shall never die. Believest thou this? 27 She saith unto him, Yea, Lord: I believe that thou art the Christ, the Son of God, which should come into the world.* Only those who have been dead can be resurrected. It was part of God's plan that Lazarus passed through death. Death was not the intended outcome, but God's timing mattered. It took the whole of this experience to bring God the full glory that was about to occur.

John 11:38-44 (KJV) *38 Jesus therefore again groaning in himself cometh to the grave. It was a cave, and a stone lay upon it. 39 Jesus said, Take ye away the stone.* Lazarus is not like Jesus and he can never come out of the grave if others do not remove the stone. *Martha, the sister of him that was dead, saith unto him, Lord, by this time he stinketh: for he hath been dead four days.* His body would have already begun to decompose. Martha is still thinking in the natural, but Jesus turns her toward the spiritual. *40 Jesus saith unto her, Said I not unto thee, that, if thou wouldest believe, thou shouldest see the glory of God?* Martha had the authority; she had to give permission to open that grave. *41 Then they took away the stone from the place where the dead was laid. And Jesus lifted up his eyes, and said, Father, I thank thee that thou hast heard me. 42 And I knew that thou hearest me always: but because of the people which stand by I said it, that they may believe that thou hast sent me.* When did the Father hear Jesus? He heard him when Jesus told the disciples that this sickness would not end in death. He also heard when Jesus said 'He sleeps but I go to wake him.' The Father heard Him when Jesus told Martha that Lazarus would live again. God the Father heard it when Jesus said, "I am the resurrection and the life." Every time Jesus spoke faith filled words about the situation was important. Jesus did not need to pray much, because His words had already laid a strong foundation for Lazarus to be resurrected. *43 And when he thus had spoken, he cried with a loud voice, Lazarus, come forth. 44 And he that was dead came forth, bound hand and foot with graveclothes: and his face was bound about with a napkin. Jesus saith unto them, Loose him, and let him go.* Jesus has been speaking faith filled words over your life. He has called you out of the dead place of your past into eternal life.

This present time is all you have. The past is over, and all that was evil in it is under the blood; it was buried in that tomb. You walked out of that tomb alive—really alive—spiritually alive for the first time. Now you are in Christ. **Acts 17:28 (KJV)** *28 For in him we live, and move, and have our being;* Because we are in Him, we live free each day. He does not want you living with regret from the past. Neither does He want you to borrow from the future with apprehension or dread.

Romans 8:15 (KJV) *15 For ye have not received the spirit of bondage again to fear; but ye have received the Spirit of adoption, whereby we cry, Abba, Father.* God is your daddy. Have confidence in that relationship. Trust that He who loved you so dearly is right there with you.

Dread is like regret; it takes you out of the present and focuses you on a time and place you can do nothing about. Trust God with all the days of your life. "I spent a lot of years with regret pulling on one arm and dread pulling on the other. The result was that I felt like I was being pulled apart, and I didn't even know what the problem was." (Meyer, p. 28) **Hebrews 11:1 (KJV)** *1 Now faith is the substance of things hoped for, the evidence of things not seen.* Not tomorrow faith or yesterday faith—now faith. We live in the present, believing for the good, not worrying about a future, but trusting the One who holds that future.

Psalm 1:1-2 (KJV) *1 Blessed is the man that walketh not in the counsel of the ungodly, nor standeth in the way of sinners, nor sitteth in the seat of the scornful. 2 But his delight is in the law of the LORD; and in his law doth he meditate day and night.* Happy and to be envied is the man who does not let anyone or anything shake him or drag him into fear, worry, dread or regret. That man is trusting in the Lord and he thinks like a free man.

Philippians 4:8 (KJV) *8 Finally, brethren, whatsoever things are true, whatsoever things are honest, whatsoever things are just, whatsoever things are pure, whatsoever things are lovely, whatsoever things are of good report; if there be any virtue, and if there be any praise, think on these things.* That is actually a good way to decide if something is worth dwelling on. Is it true? Is it honest and good and pure? Is it beautiful and does it bring hope and praise? Does it line up with what God has said in His Word? If so, give yourself to thinking about it. But if it fails the test, cast it aside. It came with a purpose; it is trying to entomb you again. He rolled the stone away, walk out of there free in spirit and mind knowing who you are in Christ.

The Hard Road

The man who walks in his own will and his own ideas of right and wrong usually finds it to be a very hard road to travel. It is the road of the rebellious and hard headed. It is a road to sorrow and want, but it always seems like such a good idea to go your own way until you are on the path.

The prodigal son is one of the best known of all the parables. It is not the story of one wayward son on the hard road, but two lost sons that were estranged from the heart of their father. God always wants to recover that which is lost. This parable concerns a wealthy, dysfunctional, upper class Jewish family.

Luke 15:11-12 (KJV) *11 And he said, A certain man had two sons: 12 And the younger of them said to his father, Father, give me the portion of goods that falleth to me.* It was not uncommon for a father to give a portion of the inheritance to his son while still living but it was at the father's discretion—it was never a choice for the heir to make. In a way, Abraham gave Isaac inheritance before his death. [See Gen. 25:5-6.] To ask for his inheritance was very rude. It was like saying, 'I wish you were dead; I don't want to wait until you die to get your stuff.' He made the money more important than their relationship. His demand was callused and cold hearted. By Jewish law he could have been stoned to death for such an open rebellion against his father. He knew that his father loved him. That gave him confidence to make the demand without fear of his Father's reaction. Obviously the son had no deep attachment to his father because he was willing to disgrace and deeply hurt his father for money. *12 And he divided unto them his living.* In a Jewish family, the eldest son got a double portion; that young rebel would have received 1/3 of the land and crops and animals as well as some money. He probably converted his share of the family estate into cash. That means that the whole town knew he dishonored his father and someone was willing to buy up his share.

Luke 15:13-16 (KJV) *13 And not many days after the younger son gathered all together, and took his journey into a far country, and there wasted his substance with riotous living.* We can see the rebellion in the heart of the boy. He did not want to work in his father's fields or follow his rules. This rebellious son wanted to have a good time, party all night, and just enjoy life. He was unconcerned about what it might cost him or his family. He was drawn to the ways of the world. After he had gone through a huge sum of money, things changed. We don't know how much time had expired. It was not recorded, but surely he was gone a while before he ran out of cash. He had become accustomed to living large. *14 And when he had spent all, there arose a mighty famine in that land; and he began to be in want.* Famine was common in those pasture lands; one or two years of bad crops and the whole nation could be hurting. He had been so wealthy that prior events like this were mostly unnoticed by his family, but he is not under the covering of his rich family now. He was now poor, destitute and in need. All his drinking buddies and girlfriends moved on to the next guy. He was alone and broke and had no great skills to land him a good job, he was in want. *15 And he went and joined himself to a citizen of that country;* He entered into a contractual relationship with a sinner, a gentile, someone who would not respect his culture or beliefs. He made himself subservient to this man. *and he sent him into his fields to feed swine. 16 And he would fain have filled his belly with the* *husks that the swine did eat: and no man gave unto him.* This is the lowest of all positions. Jews did not eat or herd pigs; they were unclean animals. If they were landowners, sometimes they had pigs that they sold to the gentiles, but they sent the lowest servants to handle the animals. They did not touch them at any time. This is so beneath his social standing and his religious convictions, but he is desperate. He not only took the job, but was at the point of eating with the swine. The pigs were usually fed carob pods. Those were long leathery pods with hard seeds inside that were somewhat sweet. They are edible but not easy to eat. The carob seeds could be ground into a powder that tasted similar to unsweetened chocolate after processing. Chewing on them without roasting or grinding would have been really difficult. This was the food of only the very poorest of the land. The pig pen is pretty much the bottom of the world's pit.

He had left because he wanted to be free, but he was in such deep bondage now. Sin is like that, tempting, and enjoyable at first. It is seemingly great freedom until it strangles its victims. **Luke 15:17-20 (KJV)** *17 And when he came to himself,* Like waking from a nightmare, he saw things in a different light. He had been morally and spiritually blind; he had not been able to see things as they really were. His sense of values had been out of balance. Now he saw his situation from the right perspective, but mostly he saw himself. He recognized he was destitute and that sin—his sin—was to blame. "This young man made the decision in that pig pen to get out of that mess and go back to his father's house, which was the direction to fulfill the purpose in his life." (Edmond, p. 134) He was ready to repent and restart. *17 And when he came to himself, he said, How many hired servants of my father's have bread enough and to spare, and I perish with hunger!* 'Even slaves and hired servants have more than I do, they don't have to beg or go to bed hungry in the gutter.' He knows he has broken fellowship with the family. He recognizes that he is the black sheep that ran from them and rejected their love. Whatever hope he has, demands that he go back and try to rebuild from the bottom. *18 I will arise and go to my father, and will say unto him, Father, I have sinned against heaven, and before* *thee,* He said, "I have sinned against heaven," that means against God Himself which is the ultimate admission of guilt. Whenever we sin and hurt another, it always damages our relationship with our true Father, God. This prodigal first sinned against God, and secondly, against his earthly father. *19 And am no more worthy to be called thy son: make me as one of thy hired servants.* Every lost soul is like him; they need to get a right perspective. There is first of all the recognition that their own sinfulness has cost them dearly. They see themselves as unworthy and unlovable. They get it that there was a price for their sin and they are continually paying that price until they change. Every sinner must, like the prodigal, recognize his fault. Return and repent! He does not expect to get reinstated in the family; he says, 'I know I violated all trust that I broke all ties, that I was hurtful and sinful and now I am coming back broken and sorrowful and needy.' He is asking for mercy. He has no rights, no hope of favor or justice; just mercy. He is hoping his father will allow him to work the land he had previously refused to work. *20 And he arose, and came to his father.*

It is one thing to feel bad about what you have done and it is another to do something about it. This boy had reached the place where it was so uncomfortable on the road of sin that he had to turn back from his rebellion. The essence of the word repentance in the Jewish language means to go home. The proper meaning is made clear here when he acted upon his sorrow. He got up and started walking, maybe a very long way. I am sure it was a hard trip. We don't know what he ate while on the trail. Maybe he had to sleep along the road where he could have encountered great danger, but finally, he made it back home.

Luke 15:20-24(KJV) *20 And he arose, and came to his father. But when he was yet a great way off, his father saw him, and had compassion, and ran, and fell on his neck, and kissed him.* Fathers didn't run; they stood and waited. But the love for his son compelled him forward. When he reached his son, it was not a well-groomed, clean son that the father wrapped his arms around. That boy had lived with the pigs and then traveled for days or weeks along a lonely road with no place to bathe and no clean clothes. Love was greater than the boy's filth, greater than his offence. *21 And the son said unto him, Father, I have sinned against heaven, and in thy sight, and am no more worthy to be called thy son.* Before he could finish the speech he had rehearsed, forgiveness and restoration came. *22 But the father said to his servants, Bring forth the best robe, and put it on him; and put a ring on his hand, and shoes on his feet: 23 And bring hither the fatted calf, and kill it; and let us eat, and be merry: 24 For this my son was dead, and is alive again; he was lost, and is found. And they began to be merry.* He had completely underestimated his father's love. The whole time this son had lived in sin, while he was far away, the father was watching for him—looking for him. This wasn't the first time he had stood looking down the road waiting and praying for his lost son to come home. That word "found" means he was searched for, longed for. If we look at the other two parables in this chapter of Luke, we see it is not the sheep that searched or the coin saying find me, it is always the owner who searched diligently for what was lost, and now the father who was wronged and rejected is seeking his lost son. "What is interesting is that the father did not know if the boy was actually coming home or not. He just loved him." (Edmond, p. 134) When his wayward son repented, the Father restored him completely—he made him as if he had never sinned. We call that justification. We call that full restoration, it was more than his son could have imagined or hoped for. He got back his position as son, with legal authority, with luxurious accommodations, and with a celebration over his return. His sin and shame were gone.

That is the story of the youngest son. The older one had issues too. The younger prodigal was the sinner and outsider. He was an outcast from the Jewish race. The elder son represents the religious Jews like the Pharisees, scribes and other devout men listening in the crowd. He was obedient but his heart was not invested in the love of the Father. The older son and the religious authorities felt they earned a reward; that their obedience made them eligible for more. They felt righteous. They had never rebelled against the law. They had not shirked their duty, had never crossed the line, and so they felt like they were better than the sinner.

If we knew more about Jewish culture, we would have picked up on the older son's issues earlier. The Jewish listener knew he was messed up from the first sentence in the parable. The eldest son was supposed to be the family mediator. In any family crisis, his job was to be loyal to the father and seek the restoration of a united family. He should have demanded that his younger brother apologize and be reconciled to his father. Because of his inaction, this older son has also failed. At the onset of the family rift, he should have acted to mend the relationship while there was still potential to stop his brother from leaving. Neither of this man's sons had a heart for their father. They both treated their father more like an employer or a banker than a loving caregiver. **Luke 15:25-28 (KJV)** *25 Now his elder son was in the field: and as he came and drew nigh to the house, he heard musick and dancing. 26 And he called one of the servants, and asked what these things meant. 27 And he said unto him, Thy brother is come; and thy father hath killed the fatted calf, because he hath received him safe and sound. 28 And he was angry, and would not go in: therefore came his father out, and intreated him.* This son humiliated his father in front of his friends and neighbors by refusing to come to the party. The father did not love him less than his younger brother, and did not ignore him. He wanted both his sons to be with him. His father wanted this son to share in the joy he felt. The Father went out to him, tried to reassure him of the love that was reserved for him. Urgently, he came to this 'good son' to draw him in. But the older son had a bad attitude too. First he had a legalistic spirit that demanded punishment, and that would crowd out mercy. He wanted the father to reject his brother, scold him and punish him, and at least make him feel shame and hurt for a season before he got any kind of forgiveness. If left up to him, his brother would not be restored and would not even have been hired on as a servant. When the father forgave and received his younger son as if there were nothing wrong, it made his older son angry, and jealous. The older son was inconsolable in his offended attitude and sense of self-righteousness.

The second problem was just plain greed. He thinks, 'That boy took his share and we are not giving him mine.' Remember it said earlier that the father divided his estate between his sons. Technically the farm is his. He feels he has some say as to what is done with the family fortune. In his heart, this young man feels to take his brother back cost him something personally. He isn't ready to forgive and forget. What is wrong with a family that wants to push others out in order to be the one shining in the spotlight? Jealousy, competition, and bitterness have no place in the family and certainly not in the church.

This older prodigal says. 'Look I am the good kid. I am righteous not like that loser brother of mine.' He tries to justify his hardness of heart. **Luke 15:29-32 (KJV)** *29 And he answering said to his father, Lo, these many years do I serve thee, neither transgressed I at any time thy commandment: and yet thou never gavest me a kid, that I might make merry with my friends:* 'It's not fair, I worked hard. I did what was right, and now you honor him. You throw a party for that sinner.' He feels no brotherly compassion; he is near hatred. *30 But as soon as this thy son was come, which hath devoured thy living with harlots, thou hast killed for him the fatted calf.* He did not want his father to forgive his brother. Honestly, he could not even bring himself to call him a brother. He said, 'That son of yours.' He is consumed with anger and self-righteousness, and self-pity. *31 And he said unto him, Son, thou art ever with me, and all that I have is thine. 32 It was meet that we should make merry, and be glad: for this thy brother was dead, and is alive again; and was lost, and is found.* The older son was so blind he did not even enjoy the full relationship he had with the father. He was the oldest and got a larger inheritance to start with. Since the boy had taken his portion when he left, the entire farm was at this son's disposal. The father tried to get him to see what really mattered. He said *"You are with me always,"* the love, the respect, the honor, and fellowship of the father was there for him the whole time. Jesus was artistically drawing a picture of life with a broken relationship. This elder son, like the Jewish elite in the crowd, was legalistic, but God wants sons who love him.

The younger prodigal was like the publicans and sinners who are obviously off track, separated by sin and believe there is little hope.

The older prodigal is walking just as hard a road because he will not let love in. Both were within the reach of their father's mercy and love. Both were wanted, but they had to choose to respond in order to walk in the joyful place that was offered to them.

When we try to focus on anything but a relationship with a loving heavenly Father, we are cheating ourselves out of the joyful inheritance He has planned for us. We make our way rock hard when we wall ourselves off from His grace. God never intended for us to focus on things or wealth or to compete with others. His love for us is perfect, and when we have strayed, He is longing for us to come home. He is watching and waiting for us to start down the path towards Him. He is running to us with arms open wide to bring us into His embrace. **Acts 2:21 (KJV)** *21 And it shall come to pass, that whosoever shall call on the name of the Lord shall be saved.* Whether you are the sinner who ran to a foreign land, or the one who resentfully acted as was expected of you, He is ready to restore you, to heal the broken places within you and fellowship with you.

Beaten, Stoned, Free

Paul surely could have lived under condemnation. Saul of Tarsus, persecutor of the church, or the Apostle Paul as we later see him said, 'I was the prodigal that stayed home, the one who judged and hated my own brothers because they were different from me and I thought they sinned.' **Acts 8:3 (KJV)** *3 As for Saul, he made havock of the church, entering into every house, and haling men and women committed them to prison.* Paul ravaged the early church. He personally arrested, jailed, and condemned to death hundreds of believers. After all that happened with Paul, he gives us a glimpse of what he saw after his redemptive reunion with the Father, and he goes on to write about two-thirds of the New Testament.

Among the truths Paul shared with the church was the fact that faith alone would save mankind, and all the hard work of the legalist never would. **Romans 9:30-33 (KJV)** *30 What shall we say then? That the Gentiles, which followed not after righteousness, have attained to righteousness, even the righteousness which is of faith. 31 But Israel, which followed after the law of righteousness, hath not attained to the law of righteousness. 32 Wherefore? Because they sought it not by faith, but as it were by the works of the law. For they stumbled at that stumblingstone; 33 As it is written, Behold, I lay in Sion a stumblingstone and rock of offence: and whosoever believeth on him shall not be ashamed.* Paul knew what he was talking about; he had tripped over that stone himself.

Saul was a religious man, a zealous Jew. He believed in the law and followed it strictly. He was so deeply entrenched in the ways of the Pharisees that he hated all those who followed Jesus. Saul was there when Stephen was attacked and killed. He watched as Stephen was stoned to death for his faith. **Acts 7:58-60 (KJV)** *58 And cast him out of the city, and stoned him: and the witnesses laid down their clothes at a young man's feet, whose name was Saul. 59 And they stoned Stephen, calling upon God, and saying, Lord Jesus, receive my spirit. 60 And he kneeled down, and cried with a loud voice, Lord, lay not this sin to their charge. And when he had said this, he fell asleep.* "Stephen forgave Saul, who consented to the martyr's stoning. Later Saul was loosed to become Paul, one of Christ's apostles and a writer of the New Testament." (Hickey, p. 17) Something happened in the spirit world that day that would eventually transform Saul, but it did not manifest for a while.

Acts 8:1 (KJV) *1 And Saul was consenting unto his death. And at that time there was a great persecution against the church which was at Jerusalem; and they were all scattered abroad throughout the regions of Judaea and Samaria, except the apostles.* Saul's hatred fueled his violent acts of religious prejudice. He hunted down and arrested the believers in Jerusalem, but even that was not enough. He wanted to drive them from the face of the earth. **Acts 9:1-4 (KJV)** *1 And Saul, yet breathing out threatenings and slaughter against the disciples of the Lord, went unto the high priest, 2 And desired of him letters to Damascus to the synagogues, that if he found any of this way, whether they were men or women, he might bring them bound unto Jerusalem. 3 And as he journeyed, he came near Damascus: and suddenly there shined round about him a light from heaven: 4 And he fell to the earth, and heard a voice saying unto him, Saul, Saul, why persecutest thou me?* Saul is on a mission to destroy every born again believer he can find, and he is intercepted by the Lord who took his assault personally. Jesus did not say, 'Why are you punishing my servants, or my children, or my church.' He said 'Why are you persecuting me?' **Acts 9: -16** *5 And he said, Who art thou, Lord? And the Lord said, I am Jesus whom thou persecutest: it is hard for thee to kick against the pricks.*

I have heard it taught that the prick was a sharp wooden spike that was placed behind the oxen that were yoked up to pull carts. If the ox was stupid and stubborn it would resist pulling and kick against it, hurting itself until it wised up and yielded to its lot in life. Here Jesus says that Saul is acting foolish and while he is arresting and jailing men of faith, it is to his own detriment. He pretty much called him a dumb ox. *6 And he trembling and astonished said, Lord, what wilt thou have me to do? And the Lord said unto him, Arise, and go into the city, and it shall be told thee what thou must do.* He did not get the full revelation that day. He was sent to the city where he fasted and prayed until God sent him more revelation. *7 And the men which journeyed with him stood speechless, hearing a voice, but seeing no man. 8 And Saul arose from the earth; and when his eyes were opened, he saw no man: but they led him by the hand, and brought him into Damascus...* At that point, God called upon one of His faithful servants to deliver a message and healing to Saul. *11 And the Lord said unto him, Arise, and go into the street which is called Straight, and enquire in the house of Judas for one called Saul, of Tarsus: for, behold, he prayeth, 12 And hath seen in a vision a man named Ananias coming in, and putting his hand on him, that he might receive his sight. 13 Then Ananias answered, Lord, I have heard by many of this man, how much evil he hath done to thy saints at Jerusalem: 14 And here he hath authority from the chief priests to bind all that call on thy name.* Ananias was not being rebellious, but he wanted to be sure God was truly leading him to go to Saul. *15 But the Lord said unto him, Go thy way: for he is a chosen vessel unto me, to bear my name before the Gentiles, and kings, and the children of Israel: 16 For I will shew him how great things he must suffer for my name's sake.*

God had a plan and a purpose for Saul to become the great man of faith that we call the apostle Paul. "On his way to Damascus Saul fell to the ground under God's power, which came in a flash of blinding light...The Lord called him into ministry right then. Sometimes I think that God may have said, Stephen didn't get to finish his work because you consented to his death. Now you get to finish it for him." (Hickey, p. 17) Paul was greatly used by God; he did not have an easy life. He was called to suffer for God just like he was called to preach. Paul could have gotten stuck in that place where his sin against the church would have consumed him. He could have lived under a black cloud of regret and shame for the rest of his life, but if he did, he would never have satisfied the call of God. "The devil will rebuke you. He will throw you on the ground and condemn you! But God will convict you and then, give you a solution with which you can overcome the problem." (Hickey, p. 50) God allows for U-turns, for second chances and for us to learn from our past and use it to bring others out of their failures.

Paul worked hard as an evangelist and teacher and church builder. He proved the truth of redemption over and over. He knew his past, he had harmed the believers, but he never let that knowledge imprison him. **1 Corinthians 15:9 (NIV)** *9 For I am the least of the apostles and do not even deserve to be called an apostle, because I persecuted the church of God.* And also, **1 Timothy 1:15 - 16 (NIV)** *15 Here is a trustworthy saying that deserves full acceptance: Christ Jesus came into the world to save sinners—of whom I am the worst. 16 But for that very reason I was shown mercy so that in me, the worst of sinners, Christ Jesus might display his unlimited patience as an example for those who would believe on him and receive eternal life.* He knew that his great sin showed the fullness of the work of redemption. He basically said, 'If God forgave me, he can forgive anyone.' God's great mercy and grace were so evident in his life that no one could deny that Christ had saved him.

There is powerful, life changing truth found in the letter to the Romans. **Romans 8:1-4 (NLT)** *1So now there is no condemnation for those who belong to Christ Jesus. 2For the power of the life-giving Spirit has freed you through Christ Jesus from the power of sin that leads to death. 3The law of Moses could not save us, because of our sinful nature. But God put into effect a different plan to save us. He sent his own Son in a human body like ours, except that ours are sinful. God destroyed sin's control over us by giving his Son as a sacrifice for our sins. 4He did this so that the requirement of the law would be fully accomplished for us who no longer follow* *our sinful nature but instead follow the Spirit.* We are not guilty because the sentence was commuted. We are set free if we will just let His spirit have reign. Paul knew first-hand about letting go of the past with all its baggage. He understood the great grace that was offered to him and partook of salvation with great zeal. He served the Lord across continents, looking for people as broken as he was, so he could to offer them new life. He no longer saw his service as adding weight to a balance against the enormity of his sin, but rather saw it as a natural response to so great a salvation.

Paul wrote most of the New Testament as letters to the churches. He taught, 'There is no longer any place of condemnation. Yes I sinned, and then I was saved. Since then, I became a new man, and because I am free I choose to tell others how to be free.' He spent his life spreading the gospel he had previously condemned. For some reason, everywhere he went, he was attacked, mocked, ridiculed and jailed but it did not silence him.

Philippians 3:12-14 (KJV) *12 Not as though I had already attained, either were already perfect: but I follow after, if that I may apprehend that for which also I am apprehended of Christ Jesus. 13 Brethren, I count not myself to have apprehended: but this one thing I do, forgetting those things which are behind, and reaching forth unto those things which are before, 14 I press toward the mark for the prize of the high calling of God in Christ Jesus.*

"When we make mistakes, as we all do, the only thing we can do is ask God's forgiveness and go on." (Meyer, p. 21) Like Paul, we learn to forget all that is in the past; we put it under the blood and go forward. "I believe Paul enjoyed his life and ministry and this 'one aspiration' of his was part of the reason why." (Meyer, p. 21) Paul let go of his past so he could press on and even though he said openly, 'I am not perfect,' he was still walking towards God and that kept him moving the right direction. When we get too focused on the past, we can't see clearly to walk forward. Never let regret wall you in or trip you up.

Paul suffered greatly for preaching the resurrected Christ. Here is one account of how he reacted to a negative situation. Paul has cast a demon out of a young woman and for his good deed he and Silas are mobbed and arrested. **Acts 16:22-26 (KJV)** *22 And the multitude rose up together against them: and the magistrates rent off their clothes, and commanded to beat them. 23 And when they had laid many stripes upon them, they cast them into prison, charging the jailor to keep them safely: 24 Who, having received such a charge, thrust them into the inner prison, and made their feet fast in the stocks. 25 And at midnight Paul and Silas prayed, and sang praises unto God: and the prisoners heard them.* Their circumstances were bad. They had been beaten and imprisoned in the lowest part of the dungeon. They were surrounded by sewage and rats but they praised God. Paul and Silas chose to respond to their circumstances by honoring God right where they were. They did not whisper their prayers or sing quietly. The Scripture says all the prisoners heard them. They were free in their hearts even when their bodies were bound. *26 And suddenly there was a great earthquake, so that the foundations of the prison were shaken: and immediately all the doors were opened, and every one's bands were loosed.* Their praise did not just set them free; it set free everyone who was bound around them. All the doors flew open, every prisoner was released.

Sometimes when you sing in your darkest hour it is for the prisoner next to you. **Acts 16:27-34 (KJV)** *27 And the keeper of the prison awaking out of his sleep, and seeing the prison doors open, he drew out his sword, and would have killed himself, supposing that the prisoners had been fled. 28 But Paul cried with a loud voice, saying, Do thyself no harm: for we are all here. 29 Then he called for a light, and sprang in, and came trembling, and fell down before Paul and Silas, 30 And brought them out, and said, Sirs, what must I do to be saved? 31 And they said, Believe on the Lord Jesus Christ, and thou shalt be saved, and thy house. 32 And they spake unto him the word of the Lord, and to all that were in his house. 33 And he took them the same hour of the night, and washed their stripes; and was baptized, he and all his, straightway. 34 And when he had brought them into his house, he set meat before them,* *and rejoiced, believing in God with all his house.* Those stone walls did not remain a prison for them; that jail became a place of revival. There were more than a few souls saved, because the prison never got inside Paul. He did not yield to fear and sorrow and anger, but rather praised God in the midst of his cell. He rejoiced in the grace of God and shared his faith in the most unlikely place for revival to break forth, and it did.

When comparing himself to other ministers he says this. **2 Corinthians 11:22-28 (KJV)** *22 Are they Hebrews? so am I. Are they Israelites? so am I. Are they the seed of Abraham? so am I. 23 Are they ministers of Christ? (I speak as a fool) I am more; in labours more abundant, in stripes above measure, in prisons more frequent, in deaths oft. 24 Of the Jews five times received I forty stripes save one. 25 Thrice was I beaten with rods, once was I stoned, thrice I suffered shipwreck, a night and a day I have been in the deep; 26 In journeyings often, in perils of waters, in perils of robbers, in perils by mine own countrymen, in perils by the heathen, in perils in the city, in perils in the wilderness, in perils in the sea, in perils among false brethren; 27 In weariness and painfulness, in watchings often, in hunger and thirst, in fastings often, in cold and nakedness. 28 Beside those things that are without, that which cometh upon me daily, the care of all the churches.* That sounds like a rather odd resume, Paul was beaten, shipwrecked, thrown into jail more times than he could count. He was actually stoned and left for dead. Through it all, he continued to preach the truth that our past sin is not greater than the gift of grace found in the cross. The old man is dead and buried in the tomb and the saved man is born again—a brand new creation.

Paul knew what John did, that once sin is forgiven it has no power. The blood of Jesus was more than enough to handle all of our sins. **1 John 1:9 (KJV)** *9 If we confess our sins, he is faithful and just to forgive us our sins, and to cleanse us from all unrighteousness.* Not just to forgive, but to put us back into a place of fellowship and blessing and usefulness. When you repent, it is not a revealing of your sin. God knew you sinned when it happened. Repentance means to turn and walk the other direction. It means you head home spiritually; there is no provision for you to carry your sin along.

When you repent, you lay your sin at the foot of the cross and walk away without it. Real repentance is a gift to every man who will call upon the name of the Lord.

1 John 3:1 - 5 (NIV) *1How great is the love the Father has lavished on us, that we should be called children of God! And that is what we are! The reason the world does not know us is that it did not know him. 2Dear friends, now we are children of God, and what we will be has not yet been made known. But we know that when he appears, we shall be like him, for we shall see him as he is. 3Everyone who has this hope in him purifies himself, just as he is pure. 4Everyone who sins breaks the law; in fact, sin is lawlessness. 5But you know that he appeared so that he might take away our sins. And in him is no sin.* We are no longer the sinner, the doubter, the murderer, we are the reborn, and restored. We are the much loved son who left as a prodigal, but has come home to a loving Father.

Paul spent years proclaiming that men could be free just as he had become free. He told everyone his story; lowly men and kings heard him say that he had been a persecutor of the church, but now he had received true salvation. He could have let his past hold him captive but instead, he used it as a starting place to build a case for grace that was greater than sin. For all his efforts he was beaten, imprisoned, and even stoned, but none of that mattered. Paul had found real freedom in knowing the Christ of Calvary, who takes all of our past, good and evil, and washes us in the blood until we are free indeed.

Striking the Rock

No matter how much God did for the Hebrews, they consistently complained. When they were in Egypt they said Moses brought additional trouble on them because they had to make brick without being provided with straw. Then they had to endure all the plagues that came—again a place to grumble. They were finally allowed to leave, but an army pursued them. God opened the Red Sea for them, and yet in just days, they were back to murmuring against God and His chosen leader. Worry, fear and discontent filled those people.

Exodus 15:22-25 (KJV) *22 So Moses brought Israel from the Red sea, and they went out into the wilderness of Shur; and they went three days in the wilderness, and found no water.* Did you notice that? This is just three days after God parted the Red Sea and drowned all of Pharaoh's army. Three days isn't very long. They could not trust a God who had done all those miracles and who was visibly present in a pillar of fire by night and a cloud by day. *23 And when they came to Marah, they could not drink of the waters of Marah, for they were bitter: therefore the name of it was called Marah. 24 And the people murmured against Moses, saying, What shall we drink?* They were angry and thirsty so they blamed their leader. *25 And he cried unto the LORD; and the LORD shewed him a tree, which when he had cast into the waters, the waters were* *made sweet: there he made for them a statute and an ordinance, and there he proved them,* The Lord showed Moses what tree to throw into the water and make it drinkable. "This wasn't the only time that God would take the bitterness out of life by using a tree. I believe that this was a type of the cross. When we apply the significance of the tree on which the Lord Jesus died to the bitterness of our life, He transforms our situation into something sweet and refreshing. (Lindsey, p.124)

Every time the children of Israel had a need, they worried and then they grumbled. We are thirsty, we are hungry, and that manna is getting boring. **Exodus 16:2-3 (KJV)** *2 And the whole congregation of the children of Israel murmured against Moses and Aaron in the wilderness: 3 And the children of Israel said unto them, Would to God we had died by the hand of the LORD in the land of Egypt, when we sat by the flesh pots, and when we did eat bread to the full; for ye have brought us forth into this wilderness, to kill this whole assembly with hunger.* When we get into a hard place sometimes we look back and think about the "good old days" before we were saved. The devil will make sure we use selective memory here so we don't remember how alone and broken and weak we were back then. Even the Bible says sin is pleasurable for a season.

In a matter of weeks, the devil had the Israelites looking longingly back to Egypt. Had they completely forgotten they were slaves there for over 400 years? Those Hebrews lived from crisis to crisis while right under the Shadow of the Almighty. They had a need and got a miracle then the next time they acted as if God had never intervened at all. They lived in a constant state of worry. "Actually, the worst sin a Christian can commit is to worry. You cannot worry and believe God's promises at the same time. Worry is the maximum expression of a lack of faith in the Lord's faithfulness and love for you." (Lindsey, p.130) Faith and worry are opposites. Either you believe that God can and will help you, or you fill your heart with doubts and fears that He will not. There is no middle ground where you can balance those two attitudes.

Exodus 17:1-6 (KJV) *1 And all the congregation of the children of Israel journeyed from the wilderness of Sin, after their journeys, according to the commandment of the LORD, and pitched in Rephidim: and there was no water for the people to drink. 2 Wherefore the people did chide with Moses, and said, Give us water that we may drink. And Moses said unto them, Why chide ye with me? wherefore do ye tempt the LORD? 3 And the people thirsted there for water; and the people murmured against Moses, and said, Wherefore is this that thou hast brought us up out of Egypt, to kill us and our children and our cattle with thirst? 4 And Moses cried unto the LORD, saying, What shall I do unto this people? they be almost ready to stone me. 5 And the LORD said unto Moses, Go on before the people, and take with thee of the elders of Israel; and thy rod, wherewith thou smotest the river, take in thine hand, and go. 6 Behold, I will stand before thee there upon the rock in Horeb; and thou shalt smite the rock, and there shall come water out of it, that the people may drink. And Moses did so in the sight of the elders of Israel.* He followed instructions and God flooded the area with drinking water from the rock.

I'm sure they were somewhat content until the next time. **Numbers 20:1-13 (KJV)** *1 Then came the children of Israel, even the whole congregation, into the desert of Zin in the first month: and the people abode in Kadesh; and Miriam died there, and was buried there. 2 And there was no water for the congregation: and they gathered themselves together against Moses and against Aaron. 3 And the people chode with Moses, and spake, saying, Would God that we had died when our brethren died before the LORD! 4 And why have ye brought up the congregation of the LORD into this wilderness, that we and our cattle should die there? 5 And wherefore have ye made us to come up out of Egypt, to bring us in unto this evil place? it is no place of seed, or of figs, or of vines, or of pomegranates; neither is there any water to drink. 6 And Moses and Aaron went from the presence of the assembly unto the door of the tabernacle of the congregation, and they fell upon their faces: and the glory of the LORD appeared unto them. 7 And the LORD spake unto Moses, saying, 8 Take the rod, and gather thou the assembly* *together, thou, and Aaron thy brother, and* <u>*speak ye unto the rock*</u> *before their eyes; and it shall give forth his water, and thou shalt bring forth to them water out of the rock: so thou shalt give the congregation and their beasts drink. 9 And Moses took the rod from before the LORD, as he commanded him. 10 And Moses and Aaron gathered the congregation together before the rock, and he said unto them, Hear now, ye rebels; must we fetch you water out of this rock?* Wait a minute that is a bad attitude I hear. 'Do I have to bring water out of the rock for you?' Moses is not focused on the God of miracles; he is discouraged and displeased and he gets in the flesh. *11 And Moses lifted up his hand, and with his rod he smote the rock twice: and the water came out abundantly, and the congregation drank, and their beasts also. 12 And the LORD spake unto Moses and Aaron, Because ye believed me not, to sanctify me in the eyes of the children of Israel, therefore ye shall not bring this congregation into the land which I have given them. 13 This is the water of Meribah; because the children of Israel strove with the LORD, and he was sanctified in them.* Moses did exactly what he had done in Exodus 17, but this time it was disobedience. He did not get them to focus on the Lord as provider, and God never said strike the rock. His moment in the flesh cost Moses dearly. Moses did not get to go into the Promised Land. Honestly, if we grumble and complain and provoke anger in our leaders, we are just like those ungrateful, stubborn, and rebellious people, and it will cost us too.

Their journey through the desert revealed what was inside them the whole time. **Deuteronomy 8:1-18 (KJV)** *1 All the commandments which I command thee this day shall ye observe to do, that ye may live, and multiply, and go in and possess the land which the LORD sware unto your fathers. 2 And thou shalt remember all the way which the LORD thy God led thee these forty years in the wilderness, to humble thee, and to prove thee, to know what was in thine heart, whether thou wouldest keep his commandments, or no. 3 And he humbled thee, and suffered thee to hunger, and fed thee with manna, which thou knewest not, neither did thy fathers know; that he might make thee know that man doth not live by bread only, but by every word that proceedeth out of the mouth of the LORD doth man live. 4 Thy raiment waxed not old upon thee, neither did* *thy foot swell, these forty years. 5 Thou shalt also consider in thine heart, that, as a man chasteneth his son, so the LORD thy God chasteneth thee. 6 Therefore thou shalt keep the commandments of the LORD thy God, to walk in his ways, and to fear him.* They had been through some stuff and most of the time they failed the faith test and yielded to murmuring and complaining. They worried and feared and grumbled. Then God, who was so gracious, still provided for them. *7 For the LORD thy God bringeth thee into a good land, a land of brooks of water, of fountains and depths that spring out of valleys and hills; 8 A land of wheat, and barley, and vines, and fig trees, and pomegranates; a land of oil olive, and honey; 9 A land wherein thou shalt eat bread without scarceness, thou shalt not lack any thing in it; a land whose stones are iron, and out of whose hills thou mayest dig brass. 10 When thou hast eaten and art full, then thou shalt bless the LORD thy God for the good land which he hath given thee. 11 Beware that thou forget not the LORD thy God, in not keeping his commandments, and his judgments, and his statutes, which I command thee this day:* That doesn't seem like the place they would fall away from God, but sometimes that is exactly what happens. While there is struggle and need, we cling to God. But once the pressure is off, we almost forget who got us this far. *12 Lest when thou hast eaten and art full, and hast built goodly houses, and dwelt therein; 13 And when thy herds and thy flocks multiply, and thy silver and thy gold is multiplied, and all that thou hast is multiplied; 14 Then thine heart be lifted up, and thou forget the LORD thy God, which brought thee forth out of the land of Egypt, from the house of bondage; 15 Who led thee through that great and terrible wilderness, wherein were fiery serpents, and scorpions, and drought, where there was no water; who brought thee forth water out of the rock of flint; 16 Who fed thee in the wilderness with manna, which thy fathers knew not, that he might humble thee, and that he might prove thee, to do thee good at thy latter end; 17 And thou say in thine heart, My power and the might of mine hand hath gotten me this wealth. 18 But thou shalt remember the LORD thy God: for it is he that giveth thee power to get wealth, that he may establish his covenant which he sware unto thy fathers, as it is this day.* Don't forget that God has done all of it. Give God the glory, and remember

His grace and kindness and tell the whole world that He is powerful and loving and draw others into a place of faith.

1 Corinthians 10:1-5 (KJV) *Moreover, brethren, I would not that ye should be ignorant, how that all our fathers were under the cloud, and all passed through the sea; 2 And were all baptized unto Moses in the cloud and in the sea; 3 And did all eat the same spiritual meat; 4 And did all drink the same spiritual drink: for they drank of that spiritual Rock that followed them: and that Rock was Christ. 5 But with many of them God was not well pleased: for they were overthrown in the wilderness.* "It is imperative to remember that our griping and complaining about life is actually griping against the Lord. And our worrying is in reality saying that the One who died for us doesn't care about us." (Lindsey, p.134)

I want to say one more thing about that verse. It says that Jesus was the Rock that consistently traveled with them in the wilderness. He was their sure foundation and so when Moses lifted up the rod and struck the rock, he was in a sense striking Jesus. Isn't that what we are doing when we rebel against God and disrespect the Lord? Are we not slapping the face of the One who promised to go with us and provide for us? When we grumble and worry and complain aren't our words an accusation against the Lord and an affront to God himself? I think they are. God responds to faith, and each time we enter into rebellion in one form or another we have taken ourselves out of faith and entered into a more selfish, fleshly attitude and it is an insult to the Lord who purchased our allegiance.

It is your responsibility to give all your cares to God and then act as if God has you covered, because He does. **1 Peter 5:7 (KJV)** *7 Casting all your care upon him; for he careth for you.* I like the Amplified Bible for this verse, it says, *"Casting the whole of your care—all your anxieties, all your worries, all your concerns, once and for all—on Him; for He cares for you affectionately, and cares about your watchfully."* Throw off that worry and fear and stress, God has you, and your life is safe in His loving hands.

Philippians 4:6-7 (NLT) *6 Don't worry about anything; instead, pray about everything. Tell God what you need, and thank him for all he has done. 7 Then you will experience God's peace, which exceeds anything we can understand. His peace will guard your hearts and minds as you live in Christ Jesus.* **Philippians 4: 19 (KJV)** *19 But my God shall supply all your need according to his riches in glory by Christ Jesus.* Trust Him! Just rest in His provision and His love, knowing He sees your every need.

Romans 8:15 (KJV) *15 For ye have not received the spirit of bondage again to fear; but ye have received the Spirit of adoption, whereby we cry, Abba, Father.* How can you let your thoughts run away with you and become ungrateful, complaining and full of discontent? How can you continue to be fearful and insecure knowing that God is your Daddy?

Hebrews 12:1-3 (ETRV) *1 We have all these great people around us as examples. Their lives tell us what faith means. So we, too, should run the race that is before us and never quit. We should remove from our lives anything that would slow us down and the sin that so often makes us fall. 2 We must never stop looking to Jesus. He is the leader of our faith, and he is the one who makes our faith complete. He suffered death on a cross. But he accepted the shame of the cross as if it were nothing because of the joy he could see waiting for him. And now he is sitting at the right side of God's throne. 3 Think about Jesus. He patiently endured the angry insults that sinful people were shouting at him. Think about him so that you won't get discouraged and stop trying.* "One of life's most difficult things is to keep on trusting the Lord when He delays answering our faith." (Lindsey, p.220) We have to keep on believing and running our race when we feel like giving up. Most of us won't be wandering in the desert for forty years. "The Lord wants us to run the spiritual race of life with an endurance that perseveres in spite of delays, obstacles, misunderstandings, and discouragements." (Lindsey, p.221) Don't let any stone in your path cause you to stumble. Choose to be useful to God and faithful no matter what stands in your way. Trust in the faithfulness of God and focus upon Him and His Word.

Isaiah 26:3-4 (KJV) *3 Thou wilt keep him in perfect peace, whose mind is stayed on thee: because he trusteth in thee. 4 Trust ye in the LORD for ever: for in the LORD JEHOVAH is everlasting strength:* Never allow yourself to become unthankful and complaining like the Hebrews that wandered in the wilderness. You may have to do some walking and some waiting, but God, who is faithful, is your Father, your provider, and He will come through for you.

Are the Rocks Crying out?

Shouts of joy filled the air as Jesus entered the city of Jerusalem. The Scripture tells us that just days before the crowds cried out for His crucifixion they shouted praises to His name. Mankind can be so fickle. The Lord entered the city triumphantly; there was great rejoicing in the streets. The religious men of the day said, 'Tell those people to be silent,' but the Lord said 'If mankind does not worship me the rocks will cry out.'

Luke 19:36-40 (KJV) *36 And as he went, they spread their clothes in the way. 37 And when he was come nigh, even now at the descent of the mount of Olives, the whole multitude of the disciples began to rejoice and praise God with a loud voice for all the mighty works that they had seen; 38 Saying, Blessed be the King that cometh in the name of the Lord: peace in heaven, and glory in the highest. 39 And some of the Pharisees from among the multitude said unto him, Master, rebuke thy disciples. 40 And he answered and said unto them, I tell you that, if these should hold their peace, the stones would immediately cry out.* Did you ever hear the rocks crying out for mercy towards us? Did you hear them shouting praise when it was given? Do you suppose the very ground that soaked up His blood shed for you rejoiced when you received His grace? If indeed, our lack of worship would cause the rocks to cry out, I want them silent. I don't want any rock to shout my praises. He is Lord, and He has saved me. He has brought me out of all the sin and guilt and regret that held me captive. How can I not praise Jesus who loved me so much He would not live without me?

I remember what it was like before I knew how very much Jesus loved me. I lived with a lot of insecurity. I remembered when I was rejected by my fiancé and then later, that same sense of rejection when my husband threatened to leave and eventually filed for divorce. I still remember feeling so unloved, and unwanted. I remember hearing these words in my spirit. "It doesn't matter who has rejected you—I accept you. If everyone else leaves, if they all turn away, I will still be here. I will always love you." God spoke those healing words into my spirit and I will never forget them. Those words pulled me out of a pit of insecurity and into a place of freedom. I will be thankful forever. I will worship Him all of my days.

It is such bondage to live in insecurity. It stops you from trying things that you really want to do. It colors your thinking with a dark sense of fear and failure. It makes you apologetic when you do less than you think the world expects. It causes you to cower at challenges. It can even make you defensive. "The trauma of insecurity manifests itself in many symptoms. Unfortunately, we struggle long with the symptoms without even suspecting their cause or origin. By spending much time in the word of God, we may conquer the symptoms one by one." (Hicks, p. 8) Insecurity can be a harsh task master; it can make you fearful, and critical. It manifests by holding you back from being who God called you to be. Our enemy uses insecurity to wall people off from their destiny in Christ.

You were saved to walk free from all insecurity. "As God our Father looks down upon us, He sees us as believers 100% pure and holy, because He sees us through the mighty sacrifice of His Son, Jesus, on the cross. In the eyes of God, a believer is as much a complete saint the day he is saved as he will ever be, whether he lives one hour or a hundred years. We cannot by works improve on our standing with God. Jesus our Lord not only died for us, shedding His precious blood for our sin, He also gave us, as a free gift, His own perfect righteousness." (Hicks, p.17) What a relief, we don't have anything to earn or anything to prove. God loves us just the way He made us. We can rejoice in that confidence. He who loved us so much will never leave us or forsake us. We stand whole and clean before Him.

Since we have such assurance of His love and acceptance, we can rejoice in our salvation. Our mouths should be filled with His praises. Only Jesus could have brought us from where we started into this new and wonderful life of salvation. Only Jesus could take those of us who were fearful and insecure and make us bold and confident. Only Jesus could take our mess and make it into a message of salvation and deliverance. No one but Jesus could ever love us so perfectly, and He deserves all our praise.

I recognize who I am today, all that is good and all that I have. I remember who He is and know that it was God in me doing what was worth remembering. I look back and see the changes He has made. Knowing how fearful and insecure and tarnished I was—I am amazed that those things no longer hold me captive. I see who I really am and who He is and praise flows forth. He who loved me so very much is with me, helping me and I love Him.

Romans 8:31-35 (NIV) *31 What, then, shall we say in response to these things? If God is for us, who can be against us? 32 He who did not spare his own Son, but gave him up for us all—how will he not also, along with him, graciously give us all things? 33 Who will bring any charge against those whom God has chosen? It is God who justifies. 34 Who then is the one who condemns? No one. Christ Jesus who died—more than that, who was raised to life—is at the right hand of God and is also interceding for us. 35 Who* *shall separate us from the love of Christ?* I read those words, and I heard the rocks falling. All the guilt and the accusations against me, every discrimination and death sentence, like stones poised in anger, dropped to the ground and were reduced to a tiny cloud of dust as my accusers fell under the pressure of their own sin in the face of such loving mercy. The shame is gone, all of my accusers have vanished and I walk confidently with the same one who said, *"Neither do I condemn thee."*

I pray that you walk free, with no hand [real or imagined] raised to throw a stone at you. I pray that you know the One who so willingly took your place, and that you are free from all condemnation. You have a God who is for you, not against you. He loves you and wants you to live to your full potential. I urge you to take seriously the words He wrote and those I have shared. May you continually rejoice in Jesus, your Savior, your Redeemer, and your Deliverer.

Works Cited

Copeland, Gloria. *God's Will For You.* (Fort Worth TX: KCP Publications,1988) p. 46, 99.

Douglas, J. D. *The New International Dictionary of the Bible.* (Grand Rapids Michigan: Zondervan Publishing House, 2011) p. 38.

Edmond, Jerry. *In Search of Purpose.* (Elgin, TX: Jerry Edmond Productions, 2016) p. 27, 28, 29, 33, 42, 77, 134.

Hagin, Kenneth Jr. *Come out of the Valley.* (Tulsa OK: Faith Library Publications, 1993) p. 4

Hickey, Marilyn. *Smooth Out Your Rough Edges: with Christ as your Carpenter.* (Denver CO: Marilyn Hickey Ministries, 1985) p. 18, 50.

Hicks, Roy. *Healing Your Insecurities.* (Tulsa, OK: Harrison House, 1982) p. 8, 17, 48, 80.

Josephus, Flavius, and William Whiston. T*he Works of Josephus: Complete and Unabridged.* (Peabody, MA: Hendrickson, 2008) p. 128.

Lindsey, Hal; *Combat Faith. (*New York: Bantam Books, 1986) p. 124, 130, 134, 220, 221.

The Living Bible Encyclopedia: In Story and Pictures. (New York: Suttman Co, 1968) p. 948-949.

Meyer, Joyce. *Enjoying Where You Are on the Way to Where You are Going: Learning to Live a Joyful Spirit-led Life.* (Tulsa, OK: Harrison House, 1996) p. 21, 28.

Treat, Casey. *Renewing the Mind: the Arena for Success:* (Tulsa, OK: Harrison House, 1984) p. 21, 22, 85.

KATHRYN L. SMITH

Author Page

I was saved in 1972, in a revival at Suburban Baptist Church in Granite City IL. I learned to love the Lord & His Word and began my walk there. In 1980 I was filled with the Holy Spirit, at Full Gospel Evangelistic Center of Alton. It was there that I began to minister the Word in Power. God called me to "build up the body of Christ," and I have been preaching and teaching all these years for that purpose. Becoming an author was a natural expansion of that call to minister. I love teaching and preaching and there is no joy greater than walking the path He places before me. I serve as an Associate Minister at The House of Victory in Cottage Hills IL, under Pastor Timothy Naylor. I am available for speaking engagements and would gladly come minister at your church or conference.

This is the third book I have written. If you enjoyed this one please think about reading my other two. <u>There is Fire in the Blood</u>, my first book, explores the blood sacrifices throughout time as they point to the Blood of Jesus and bring us the Fire of His presence. It was the same fire that fell on the sacrificial altars of Abel, Elijah, and Moses that produced the blaze of Pentecost. As we honor the Blood and recognize its power we make way for the glory of God; if we want to experience the Fire, we know where to find it; 'There is Fire in the Blood.'

My second book, <u>Meet Me on the Mountain</u>, focuses on intimate fellowship with God. The mountain of God is that place where faith and hunger and obedience produce His presence. The drive to climb is not just man striving for God; it is an answer to the call. God loved us first and He is calling to the heart of man to draw nearer and stay longer in His presence. This book has more personal experiences included to demonstrate how He meets with us and longs for passionate fellowship with His children. If you seek Him—you will find Him.

Contact information:
Fire in the Blood Ministries
Rev. Kathy Smith
Email: klssaved1972@yahoo.com
Fire in the Blood Ministries also has a Facebook Page
fbm/revkathy   or   m.me/revkathy

I Hear the Rocks Falling

KATHRYN L. SMITH

www.ingramcontent.com/pod-product-compliance
Lightning Source LLC
Chambersburg PA
CBHW071522080526
44588CB00011B/1524